D0153266

The Tainted War

Recent Titles in
Contributions in Military Studies

The Tainted War

Culture and Identity
in Vietnam War Narratives

LLOYD B. LEWIS

Contributions in Military Studies, Number 44

Greenwood Press
Westport, Connecticut · London, England

Library of Congress Cataloging in Publication Data

Lewis, Lloyd B.
   The tainted war.

   (Contributions in military studies, ISSN 0883-6884 ;
no. 44)
   Bibliography: p.
   Includes index.
   1. Vietnamese Conflict, 1961–1975—Personal
narratives, American.   2. Vietnamese Conflict, 1961–1975—
Social aspects—United States.   3. Vietnamese Conflict,
1961–1975—Psychological aspects.   I. Title.   II. Series.
DS559.5.L49   1985   959.704′31   84-27926
ISBN 0-313-23723-9 (lib. bdg.)

Copyright © 1985 by Lloyd B. Lewis

All rights reserved. No portion of this book may be
reproduced, by any process or technique, without the
express written consent of the publisher.

Library of Congress Catalog Card Number: 84-27926
ISBN: 0-313-23723-9
ISSN: 0883-6884

First published in 1985

Greenwood Press
A divison of Congressional Information Service, Inc.
88 Post Road West
Westport, Connecticut 06881

Printed in the United States of America

10 9 8 7 6 5 4 3 2 1

Copyright Acknowledgments

CONVERSATIONS WITH AMERICANS by Mark Lane. Copyright © 1970
by Mark Lane. Reprinted by permission of SIMON & SCHUSTER, Inc.

From DISPATCHES, by Michael Herr. Copyright © 1977 by Michael Herr.
Reprinted by permission of Aldred A. Knopf, Inc, for publication in the
United States, its dependencies, the Philippine Republic, Canada, and
elsewhere except the British Commonwealth (excluding Canada).

Quotations from DISPATCHES by Michael Herr. Copyright © 1977 by
Michael Herr. Reprinted by permission of Candida Donadio & Associates,
British Commonwealth (excluding Canada).

Quotations from EVERYTHING WE HAD: AN ORAL HISTORY OF THE
VIETNAM WAR BY THIRTY-THREE AMERICAN SOLDIERS WHO

LIBRARY
ALMA COLLEGE
ALMA, MICHIGAN
FOUGHT THERE by Al Santoli. Copyright © 1981 by Al Santoli. Reprinted by permission of Random House, Inc.

From the book FIELDS OF FIRE by James Webb. Copyright © 1978 by James Webb. Published by Prentice-Hall, Inc., Englewood Cliffs NJ 07632. Permission granted to reprint throughout the United States, Canada and the Phillipines by Prentice-Hall, Inc. Permission to reprint throughout all other territories by James Webb.

Quotes excerpted from the book IF I DIE IN A COMBAT ZONE: Box Me Up and Ship Me Home by Tim O'Brien. Copyright © 1973 by Tim O'Brien. Reprinted by permission of DELACORTE PRESS/SEYMOUR LAWRENCE.

Excerpt from M by John Sack. Copyright © 1966, 1967 by John Sack. Reprinted by permission of the author.

About 3,300 words, as scattered quotes, from NAM by Mark Baker. Copyright © 1981 by Mark Baker. By permission of William Morrow & Company, for publication in the United States, its dependencies, Philippine Islands, Canada, and all territory outside the British Commonwealth.

Quotations from NAM by Mark Baker. Copyright © 1981 by Mark Baker. Reprinted by permission of International Creative Management for publication in the United States and the rest of the world.

Several brief quotations from ONE VERY HOT DAY by David Halberstam. Copyright © 1967 by David Halberstam. Reprinted by permission of Houghton Mifflin Company, for rights in the United States and Canada.

Selected extracts from ONE VERY HOT DAY by David Halberstam. Copyright © 1967 by David Halberstam. Reprinted by permission of International Creative management, for publication throughout the world.

From a RUMOR OF WAR by Philip Caputo. Copyright © 1977 by Philip Caputo. Reprinted by permission of Holt, Rinehart and Winston, Publishers, for publication in the United States, its territories and dependencies, the Philippines and Canada. Permission for publication in the British Commonwealth (except Canada) granted by the Aaron Priest Literary Agency.

Quotations from Peter L. Berger and Thomas Luckmann: THE SOCIAL CONSTRUCTION OF REALITY (Penguin University Books 1971). Copyright © Peter L. Berger and Thomas Luckmann, 1966. Reprinted by permission of Penguin Books Ltd for distribution rights in the British (excluding Canada) market, in the English language.

Excerpt from THE SOCIAL CONSTRUCTION OF REALITY by Peter Berger and Thomas Luckmann. Copyright © 1966 by Peter Berger and Thomas Luckmann. Reprinted by permission of Doubleday & Company, Inc.

Quotations from WINNERS AND LOSERS: BATTLES, RETREATS, GAINS, LOSSES, AND RUINS FROM A LONG WAR by Gloria Emerson. Copyright © 1973 by Gloria Emerson. Reprinted by permission of Random House, Inc.

To the memory of Gene Wise (1936–1983)
scholar, teacher, and friend

Contents

Foreword

The Vietnam War was 'the big taint'—T'aint reality, and t'aint a dream.

> —Former Marine sniper
> *The Washington Post Magazine*
> June 25, 1983, p. 7

No event in recent American history proved more traumatic to the American people than the Vietnam War, and no group of Americans suffered that trauma longer or more intensely than the young men who witnessed it firsthand: the ground troops participating in combat operations. This study endeavors to reconstruct, from their own accounts, the world view of these soldiers. Their responses illuminate both the nature of that unprecedented military disaster and the larger cultural forces that made it possible.

Chapter 1, "Propaedeutic," sets forth the assumptions that undergird this study. These assumptions belong to the sociology of knowledge as that field has been redefined in recent years. This theoretical sub-discipline of sociology provides the conceptual tools for a thoroughgoing analysis of the processes through which social reality is constructed and subjectively appropriated by individuals.

The social reality, or "symbolic universe," shared by a generation of American males sent to war in Southeast Asia is described in Chapter 2, "Initiation." An analysis of that symbolic universe (and the mechanisms by which it was transmitted from one generation to the next) reveals that Americans were socialized to think of warfare in terms borrowed exclusively from the Second World War.

The consequences of this dysfunctional socialization are explored in Chapter 3, "The Retreat from Meaning." Under the actual combat conditions in Vietnam—an unconventional jungle war—the Americans found themselves compelled to scrap the cultural knowledge they had been taught. They thereupon adopted a belief system giving priority to sheer physical survival. The result was the collapse of traditional military beliefs, e.g., duty, honor, discipline, valor. An important social consequence of this "retreat from meaning" was the empowerment of alternative institutional arrangements to confer meaning upon experience.

Chapter 4, "Walking Wounded," analyzes the effects of these institutional supports being withdrawn during the individual's rapid transition from combat soldier to civilian. The veterans' difficult post-war adjustment to civilian life involves the debilitating social recognitions to which they were subjected. These recognitions bestowed social identities which left the soldiers in a cultural twilight zone.

The "Afterword" draws some conclusions from the Vietnam veterans' experiences and suggests that the "lessons of Vietnam" include a sociological, as well as a geopolitical, dimension.

Preface

There is no novel in Nam, there is not enough for a plot, nor is there really any character development. If you survive 365 days without getting killed or wounded you simply go home again and take up where you left off.

—*365 Days*, p. 64

Things happened, things came to an end. There was no sense of developing drama.

—*If I Die in a Combat Zone*, p. 17

The incidents I do remember, I remember vividly; but I can come up with no connecting thread to tie events neatly together.

—*A Rumor of War*, p. 90

No war is entirely unique. In a generic sense, the Vietnam and Peloponnesian Wars are identical. They both entail "the sanctioned use of lethal weapons by members of one society against members of another."[1] Commentators describing both conflicts have recognized this fact. In 432 B.C. Thucydides wrote, "The lack of the fabulous may make my work dull. But I shall be satisfied if it be thought useful by those who wish to know the exact character of events past which, human nature being what it is, will recur in similar or analogous form."[2] Twenty centuries later his counterpart, Michael Herr, observed that "somewhere on the periphery of that total Vietnam issue whose daily reports made the morning papers too heavy to bear, lost in the surreal contexts of television, there was a story as simple as it had always been: men hunting men, a hideous war and all kinds of victims."[3] Clearly, peacemongering has no firmer hold in the modern world than it had in the ancient.

Nevertheless, the Vietnam War is unusual in certain respects. Geopolitically, the Vietnam War stands out as a counterinsurgency conflict undertaken by an advanced industrial society against a revolutionary movement of an underdeveloped country. This fact, arresting in its own right and worthy of extended policy postmortem, is peripheral to the analysis that follows. Of utmost importance, in contrast, is that a significant number of those who actually fought the Vietnam War rejected the conventional image of noble killing and insisted upon calling it collective murder. This rejection distinguishes the Vietnam War from the one waged two thousand years earlier and renders it exceptional in American, although not modern, military history.[4] It also motivates this study.

The question we shall endeavor to answer in the following pages is: *How did the Vietnam War defy interpretation as meaningful combat ritual?* An anecdote from the Vietnam War narratives may help to clarify this issue. An officer, preparing his troops for battle, delivered the following address: "I don't know why I'm here. You don't know why you're here. But since we're both here, we might as well try to do a good job and do our best to stay alive."[5] That speech amounts to a recognition, even a resigned acceptance, of anti-meaning: the unintelligibility of experience using customary interpretive schema.

It is our purpose to explain the conditions necessary to produce such a recognition and to explore the consequences of having held it . By so doing, we intend to convey something of the subjective reality of the experience. This task involves a diachronic movement through successive stages of conviction, doubt, and restructured belief. That is the plan of organization that informs this study. We begin by examining widely shared certainties, trace their deterioration, and conclude with an assessment of the new assumptions arising from that encounter between mind and world. There is no convenient symbol to represent the psychic costs incurred in that involuted process. The phrase which serves as the title of this study, therefore, is simply convenient metaphor. Its sole merit lies in its original usage by the participants to denote the particular perceptions under consideration.

The attempt to answer the question we have posed inevitably raises others. Specifically, an investigation into the processes whereby meanings become obsolescent implies an understanding of the way stable meaning is sustained normally. Moreover, the nature of the data from which this thesis of bankrupt meaning is derived must be distinguished. The propaedeutic that follows should serve to resolve those preliminary problems.

NOTES

1. Anthony F. C. Wallace, "Psychological Preparations for War," in *War: The Anthropology of Armed Aggression*, ed. Morton Fried, Marvin Harris, and Robert Murphy (Garden City, N.Y.: The Natural History Press, 1968), p. 173.

2. Thucydides, *The Peloponnesian Wars*, trans. John H. Finley, Jr. (New York: Random House, 1951), p. 234.

3. Michael Herr, *Dispatches* (New York: Alfred A. Knopf, 1978), p. 214.

4. One striking example of a group of war veterans whose narratives echo those of our Vietnam warriors are the German frontsoldiery of WWI. Their experience was structurally similar to that of our population of Vietnam vets in several telling respects: employing a perversely unintelligible military strategy, battling an often faceless foe, prosecuting a war whose aims remained incomprehensible, and, most crucially, returning to a society in which they were denominated "losers" and subjected to rituals of shame and humiliation including the observance of a suffocating silence. A thorough exposition of these soldiers' travails which sheds light on their similarity with the combatants treated in this study may be found in Eric J. Leed, *No Man's Land* (Cambridge: Cambridge University Press, 1979). I should like to thank Professor Leed for reading this study while in manuscript and offering helpful suggestions.

5. Robert Jay Lifton, *Home from the War* (New York: Simon and Schuster, 1973), p. 40.

Acknowledgments

Any work of scholarship—especially one that claims interdisciplinary relevance—is the product of various influences. This one is no exception. Therefore I should like to thank the following faculty members of the American Studies Department of the University of Maryland:

R. Gordon Kelly for teaching me to read literary texts as historical documents;
Gene Wise for teaching me to read historical documents as literary texts; and
John Caughey for teaching me that ethnography like charity, begins at home.

Any scholar—especially one that aspires to lead a life as well as a life of the mind—is the product of various influences. This one is no exception. Therefore I should like to thank the following members of my (extended) family:

Patricia L. Bowden for her faith in me and sobering commonsense;
Steven G. Koster for sticking around for thirty years through thick and thin;
Dr. Chauncey W. Bowers for, in Cicero's words, his "knowledge of things human and divine and of the causes by which these things are controlled";

Nancy J. Bell for showing me the ropes and then enabling me to untangle myself from them;

Dr. Heather P. Kurent for her inspiring example of personal bravery at dissertation time;

Dr. Ronald F. Lewis for bearing the burdens of brotherhood; and Pearl Leopard (UM) and Diane Walker (UT-D) for typing admist my griping.

Abbreviations of Selected Vietnam War Narratives

COW	*Casualties of War*
CWA	*Conversations with Americans*
D	*Dispatches*
EWH	*Everything We Had*
FF	*Fields of Fire*
FFZ	*Free-Fire Zone*
Fr. F.	*Friendly Fire*
GAC	*Going after Cacciato*
HFW	*Home from the War*
IID	*If I Die in a Combat Zone*
KZ	*The Killing Zone*
N	*Nam*
VHD	*One Very Hot Day*
RW	*A Rumor of War*
ST	*The Short-Timers*
3D	*365 Days*
TNL	*The New Legions*
WL	*Winners and Losers*
WUF	*Writing under Fire*

The Tainted War

1

Propaedeutic: The Sociology of Knowledge and the Vietnam War Narratives

Many social scientists have turned away from a laws-and instances ideal of explanation toward a cases-and-interpretations one. . . . The move toward conceiving of social life as organized in terms of symbols whose meaning we must grasp if we are to understand that organization and formulate its principles, has grown by now to formidable proportions.

—Clifford Geertz

The basic contentions of the argument developed in this study are drawn from the sociology of knowledge. Although that subfield of sociological analysis has appeared in a number of forms in both its homeland, Germany, and in America, the distinction between its original formulation and a latter redefinition of the field will clarify the theoretical underpinnings of the argument presented here.

The phrase "the sociology of knowledge" is most often identified with the name of Karl Mannheim. His pioneering work *Ideology and Utopia* remains the most widely known study in the discipline a half century after its appearance in English.[1] Like the work of his predecessor, Max Scheler, who first coined the phrase, Mannheim's thought stands squarely in the Germanic, "classical" tradition of the sociology of knowledge. This tradition, as the title of Mannheim's *magnum opus* suggests, concerned itself with "knowledge" and its social determinants almost exclusively in the Marxian sense of "false consciousness." As a consequence, the fledgling discipline became mired in political and epistemological issues of a decidedly non-empirical cast. The former led to the postulation of a *freischwebende Intelligenz*, a "freely-poised intelligentsia" immune to class interests, the latter to the concept of *relationism* as a counter to the problems posed by relativism and the possibility of objective knowledge.[2] These concepts, while of considerable historical significance for grasping the intellectual ferment of Germany in the 1920s, perform no useful social scientific function.

In America, the hegemony of the structural-functionalist school within sociology offered an inhospitable intellectual climate for the rehabilitation of the sociology of knowledge along more theoretically rigorous lines. While both Robert Merton and Talcott Parsons, the "deans" of the structural-functionalist school, acknowledge this approach, neither attempts to integrate it into his own thinking.[3] Both regard the sociology of knowledge as peripheral, a sub-specialty of European provenance concerned solely with the role of ideas. Given the basic tenets of the structural-functionalist perspective, especially its antipathy to "the idealist tradition" in Continental thought, they understood that role as secondary, if not negligible.[4]

This study relies upon a relatively recent reformulation of the sociology of knowledge which envisions a dialectically causal role for ideas (in an extended and specialized sense of "idea"). This is the phenomenological school founded by the German Alfred Schutz and developed by an American disciple, Peter L. Berger (and the latter's revolving staff of co-authors: Brigitte Berger, Hansfried Kellner, Thomas Luckmann, Dennison Nash, Richard J. Neuhaus, and Stanley Pullberg). Schutz's sociology of knowledge circumvents the major pitfalls of the "classical" tradition which contributed to its segregation from mainstream American sociology. Avoiding the temptation to a history of ideas approach on the one hand and an epistemologically philosophical approach on the other, Schutz retained the fundamental Marxian insight which gave rise to the field initially, namely that "man's consciousness is determined by his social being."[5] Following Schutz, Berger develops a systematic sociology of knowledge capable of steering between the Scylla of socially distorted thought ("false consciousness") and the Charybdis of meta-social "truth" (positivist science) by focusing on the Schutzian problematic: *the reality of everyday life.*

Schutz insisted that everyday life was "the paramount reality" because of its subjective relevance for members of any society.[6] The problem of the relationship between ideas and their social context could therefore be more fruitfully approached by "bracketing" questions of truth and falsity in order to illuminate the foundations of thought in everyday life. This bracketing procedure yields the purely descriptive method of phenomenological analysis. Such a method takes as "given" the subjective experience of everyday life for which its mode of explanation is designed.

A sociology of knowledge thus conceived has several advantages. Most importantly, the primary emphasis of the discipline is no longer on theoretical "ideas" as privileged social phenomena. Commonsense thinking, knowledge in the broadest sense, structures the world of everyday life. Hence, pretheoretical (or non-theoretical) thought is the appropriate object of analysis because it serves as the general framework within which more narrow "intellectualizing" occurs. An adequate understanding of the latter depends upon a thorough grasp of the former. The Schutzian problematic renders ideas, and especially ideology, parts of a larger domain: the Lebenswelt or "life-world" of the members of a society. In Berger's words, "common-sense 'knowledge' rather than 'ideas' . . . constitutes the fabric of meanings without which no society could exist."[7]

Moreover, "this far-reaching re-definition of the nature and scope" of the sociology of knowledge "moves it from the periphery to the very center of sociological theory" by challenging the structural-functionalist orthodoxy reigning in America since the decline of "the Chicago School" of the 1920s.[8] Drawing upon Schutz's work on typification as the basis of institutionalization, Berger argues forcefully that social institutions need not be conceptualized as functionally integrated. The "systems" analyzed by structural-functionalists as underlying

realities of social order are *ascribed* (not described) properties
of society—more or less ad hoc theories of varying degrees of
intellectual sophistication superimposing cohesiveness upon the
institutional order. In Marxian terms, structural-functional-
ism reifies social phenomena by bestowing upon it an ontological status independent of human thought and action.

In contrast, Berger maintains that the social world, including institutions, is constituted by specific sorts of common-
sense knowledge: generalizations, typifications, forms, categories, meanings. It is only through meanings that human
beings experience, understand, and manipulate themselves and
each other. Because these meanings are shared, i.e., social, the
study of society necessarily involves the study of meanings. In
response to the reifying tendencies of structural-functional-
ism, Berger contends that "only by way of the detour of socially shared universes do we arrive at the need for institutional integration."[9] This "detour," in fact, comprises the
sociological enterprise as Berger conceives it.

Specifically, Berger understands the task of the sociology of
knowledge as elucidating the social processes in and through
which "subjective meanings become objective facticities." These
processes, taken together, Berger calls "the social construction of reality"—the production, maintenance, and modification of the symbolic universes inhabited by human beings.
These symbolic universes are constructed through a continuing dialectic of externalization/objectivation/internalization.
Each of these can be thought of as a "moment" corresponding,
respectively, to the statements "society is a human product;
society is an objective reality; man is a social product."[10]

This dialectical view renders any discussion of "human nature" in the sense of an unvarying anthropological essence
largely beside the point. "There is no human nature in the sense
of a biologically fixed substratum determining the variability
of socio-cultural formations. . . . While it is possible to say that
man has a nature, it is more significant to say that man con-
structs his own nature, or more simply, that man produces
himself."[11] Human biology figures only in the first "moment"
of this self-production: externalization. Because of man's biological equipment, "human being must ongoingly externalize

itself. . . . These biological facts serve as the necessary presupposition for the production of social order."[12] Externalization, then, compels socio-cultural processes but does not directly determine their form.

Objectivation refers to the "moment" in which products of externalization (human activity) become available both to their producers and to other men as objects of a common world. These products can serve to indicate subjective processes and therefore make meanings sharable. Objectivations give spatio-temporal substance to subjective meanings. Anger, for instance, can be objectivated by means of a weapon. The most significant example of objectivation is human language, which, like a weapon, enables subjectivity to become stabilized and generally available as empirical fact, "reality." Unlike the weapon, however, language is explicitly significatory and may have no "instrumental" value. Its importance lies precisely in this feature. For social reality is objectivated primarily through linguistic means. By subsuming particular experiences under general categories, language renders them part of the stock of cultural knowledge. Language also serves as the principal instrumentality of "legitimation," the process whereby an objectivation is explained and justified. For instance, warfare is often legitimated by the promise of the perdurable peace it will bring. One notable instance of this particular legitimating strategy is President William McKinley's assertion, "We go to war only to make peace. We never went to war with any other design. We carry the national conscience wherever we go." Objectivations (and the legitimations that support them) thus constitute the reality shared by members of a society.

The third "moment," internalization, is the process whereby an individual interprets an objectivation as expressing meaning. Through internalization, one apprehends another's subjectivity. In humans, internalization is most apparent during primary socialization as parents, "significant others," filter objectivations to the infant. By internalizing these objectivations, the infant acquires an identity and locates it in a wider social reality. As Berger insists, "identity is objectively defined as location in a certain world and can be subjectively appropriated only along with that world."[13] During primary socialization, the child internalizes society most completely by learning to substitute "the generalized other" for the significant other as the source of cognitive and normative guidelines for conduct. This process, depending decisively on the acquisition of language, enables the child to "know" that "x is the case," rather than that "Mommy *says* x is the case." In short, primary socialization is the site of internalization par excellence because of the high degree of certainty in which the objectivations filtered to the child are held.

The process of internalization continues throughout the individual's life span in secondary socialization. Through learning sequences that are socially defined, the member of society masters relevant bodies of knowledge that are differentially distributed socially. In American culture, for example, the latter part of one's teenage years is considered ideal for teaching lower-class males the rudiments of modern warfare, although that same period is deemed suitable for introducing middle- and upper-class boys to the mysteries of a liberal arts education. In both instances, a high level of certainty in the objectivations presented by the secondary socializing agencies can be achieved.

The result of these three "moments" (the continual use of quotation marks is intended to emphasize their simultaneity, despite the term's connotation of temporal sequence) is a measure of symmetry between objective and subjective reality: a single reality in which what is real "outside" corresponds to what is real "within." The nineteen-year-old American male of lower-class origins understands his feelings of patriotism to be as real as his M–16 rifle. His upper-class counterpart feels similarly about his love of poetry in relation to his dog-eared copy of *The Waste Land*. The social worlds of both individuals are constituted by meanings, each with specific provenance, authority, and consequences. An understanding of Advanced Infantry Training on the one hand or an Advanced Poetry Seminar on the other demands consideration of the meanings assigned to happenings in each. The sociology of knowledge, as reformulated by Berger and his colleagues, provides the theoretical basis for that consideration.

This brief sketch of a complex and demanding argument in

its historical context can hardly do it full justice. The point is that "the worlds inhabited by men can be conceptualized as structured systems of shared meaning, specific to a certain time and place, and consensually maintained."[14] Such a view of society implies two questions: What do members of a particular social world believe? And why do they hold such beliefs? The purpose of this study is to answer those questions with respect to the world of the American combat infantryman in Vietnam during the decade comprising "The Second Indochina War."[15]

The theoretical claims of this study are, therefore, extremely modest. We neither refine nor extend the theory advanced by Berger, et al. Findings from other schools of cultural analysis compatible with the sociology of knowledge are adduced to buttress the argument where applicable. The social psychology of George Herbert Mead, symbolic anthropology of Clifford Geertz, and micro-sociology of Erving Goffman figure prominently at various points. Such opportunistic eclecticism hardly amounts to theoretical syncretism. That is a task best left to sociological model builders—creatures possessed by altogether different demons.[16]

Empirically, however, this study attempts to redress an imbalance of some proportions. If, as C. Wright Mills has charged, mainstream American sociology is guilty of producing a plethora of "molecular work," micro-studies of ever diminishing relevance to a general consideration of social phenomena,[17] the sociology of knowledge originated by Schutz has exhibited precisely the opposite defect. The level of abstraction employed by Berger to clarify "the processes by which any body of 'knowledge' comes to be socially established as 'reality,'"[18] places him in continual jeopardy of losing sight of his subject: people in an historically created society. The trans-historical and pan-cultural breadth of his theory often obscures this human dimension.

Although understandable as a heuristic strategy, many of Berger's illustrations are drawn from a world of empirically unavailable social situations. For instance, he often conjures up a Crusoe and Friday socially constructing a reality *de novo* on an unnamed island in an unspecifiable time. Equally intangible (and unlikely) is his paradigm population of A, B, and C whose interesting sexual exploits do not quite bestow upon them the distinctive features to which a humanistic sociology must attend. In fairness to Berger, it must be remarked that he anticipates such criticism and acknowledges that "apart from stimulating sociological fantasies, such heuristic fictions are useful only insofar as they help to clarify the conditions that favor approximations to them."[19] Such clarification, however, can also be achieved by replacing bloodless abstractions with actual people grounded in the exigencies of history: American males learning war in the United States in the 1950s, practicing it in Asia in the 1960s, and suffering its aftermath in the 1970s and 1980s.

This study takes its central task from an agenda set by Berger for the redefined sociology of knowledge he has proposed. He concludes his central theoretical work by observing that "empirical research into the relation of institutions to symbolic universes will greatly enhance the sociological understanding of contemporary society."[20] We therefore offer a "socio-cultural" interpretation of Vietnam War narratives, concerned with both social structure (institutions) and culture (symbolic universes). The following assumptions inform such an approach:

1. Belief systems are cultural in nature. Belief is an aggregate phenomena that requires explanation in aggregate terms.

2. Belief systems exist in two social contexts, a context of meaning and a context of social organization; unless both of these contexts are understood, beliefs are not intelligible.

3. The explanation for the rise and change of belief systems lies in the fact that they have utility in group adaptation to strain or disorder.[21]

These assumptions dictate that we tack back and forth between cognitive processes and the social forms in which they are collectively embodied.

Texts and Tactics

> Can the foot soldier teach anything important about war, merely for having been there? I think not. He can tell war stories.
>
> *—If I Die in a Combat Zone*, p. 32

> War stories aren't really anything more than stories about people, anyway.
>
> *—Dispatches*, p. 245

The nature of the data upon which this two-pronged "socio-cultural" interpretation rests requires some elucidation. The sociology of knowledge perspective is applied in this study to personal narrative accounts—"stories"—of the men who fought in the Vietnam War. These stories range from the barely articulate offhand remarks, full of ellipses, of troops just in from combat operations to the carefully crafted fictions of machine-gunners-turned-professional-writers. Most emphatically, literary merit was not among the criteria used to determine inclusion in this study.

In fact, this study assumes that there is no such thing as "literature" in the sense of aesthetic properties inherent to texts. This sense, dependent upon a relatively recent mode of perceiving verbal artifacts, has been distortive in a manner illuminated by the sociology of knowledge perspective: it reifies certain human products by placing them in an ontic realm apart from human activity. Perhaps the most extreme instance of such reification is Northrop Frye's well-known assertion that "poems, like poets, are born, and not made."[22] In the face of such mystification, it is useful to remember that

literature has no independent essence, aesthetic or otherwise. It is an arbitrary classification of linguistic works which do not exhibit common distinctive traits, and which cannot be defined as an Aristotelian species. Aesthetic categories are intrinsic to aesthetic *inquiries*, but not to the nature of literary works.[23]

A socio-cultural inquiry can profitably bracket the issue of evaluative criteria for texts. To avoid unnecessary confusion between the descriptive and evaluative connotations of the term "literature," we have eschewed its use. The linguistically neutral "narrative" is employed in its stead. We assume, with Clifford Geertz, that

the properties connecting texts with one another, that put them, ontologically anyway, on the same level, are coming to seem as important in characterizing them as those dividing them; and rather than face an array of natural kinds, fixed types surrounded by sharp qualitative differences, we more and more see ourselves surrounded by an almost continuous field of variously intended and diversely constructed works we can order only practically, relationally, and as our purposes prompt us.[24]

For that reason, no attempt has been made to distinguish between the various genres appropriate to conventional literary discourse. The distinction between "factual" and "fictional" narrative has been purposely overlooked in some instances. The sociology of knowledge perspective renders such a distinction a refusal to "bracket" questions of epistemological validity. The strength of phenomenological method lies in its insistence on the "constructedness" of all interpretations of reality. The degree of constructedness need not concern us here.[25] This means that some first-person narratives traditionally segregated on the basis of their epistemological claims have been incorporated as cultural evidence: autobiographies, novels, interviews, memoirs, short stories, oral histories, new journalism articles, and bits of linguistic behavior that one correspondent describes as "hardly stories at all but sounds packed with so much urgency that they became more dramatic than a novel, men talking in short violent bursts as though they might not get to finish" (D, p. 30).

Although we have not discriminated amongst these stories generically, a principle of selection does inform this study. The multiplicity of social worlds of American servicemen dictates a criterion based on the overtly social features of military rank and military role. First, the narrators treated in this study were

company-grade officers *and below*. The vast majority were enlisted personnel and Non-Commissioned Officers (NCOs). Field-
grade officers (majors and colonels) and generals have been
excluded for reasons most succinctly offered by one war correspondent: "In most organizations it is the permanent long-
standing members who usually take on the most critical tasks;
the more transient and less-skilled members are relegated to
support roles. But not so in the Army during the Vietnam War.
There the 'regulars' did less of the fighting than the amateurs
who had been pressed into the enterprise against their will"
(*WL*, p. 254). Professional military men as a group tend to
portray the Vietnam War in terms quite unlike those employed by their inferiors in rank. For instance, in *A Soldier
Reports*, General William Westmoreland insists that the war
could have been won if the U.S. had acted "decisively" (a favorite word in the upper reaches of the officer corps) at the
outset instead of following a policy of escalation. That memoir
has been described by one able historian as "bland and defensive."[26] Whatever the accuracy of the General's judgment concerning civilian "interference" (another favorite word), his position betrays a concern with conditions far removed from those
occupying the minds of his combat troops.

Second, these lower-echelon ground troops experienced the
war much differently than did sailors or fliers. The "grunts"
wading through rice paddies or hacking through jungle confronted guerilla warfare in a way their comrades flying above
it or sailing around it could not. Moreover, although 2,300,000
men served in Vietnam over a twelve-year period, "only one
in twenty saw combat, others typed or cooked, made charts or
bar graphs, trained dogs or answered phones, were clerk-typ-
ists and mechanics, did laundry or maintained aircraft. They
did not do the killing, they only made it possible" (*WL*, p. 10).
The subject of this study, therefore, is the less than 5 percent
of all the GIs connected with the tragedy of Vietnam.

By defining a population of narrators this way, we achieve
fairly precise parameters delimiting the social world under
consideration. The narrators offer two group portraits corresponding roughly to the "socio-cultural" categories between
which this interpretation oscillates. The first specifies certain

demographic features: "Most of the men were unable to capitalize on college draft deferments. A majority had enlisted. Nearly half their fathers were blue-collar workers" (*WL*, p. 332). The second isolates particular cultural assumptions: "A few generalizations can be made about all of them. They were to a man thoroughly American, in their virtues as well as flaws: idealistic, insolent, generous, direct, violent, and provincial in the sense that they believed the ground they stood on was now forever a part of the United States simply because they stood on it" (*RW*, p. 26).

These then, are the narrators whose words appear in quotation marks throughout this study. By attending to these words, we shall, as Clifford Geertz urges, "descend into detail, past the misleading tags, past the metaphysical types, past the empty similarities to grasp firmly the essential character of not only the various cultures but the various sorts of individuals within each culture, to encounter humanity face to face." The purpose of any such encounter, of the study of culture in all its myriad forms, is "to make available to us answers that others have given, and thus to include them in the consultable record of what man has said."[27]

NOTES

1. Karl Mannheim, *Ideology and Utopia*, trans. Louis Wirth and Edward Shils (London: Routledge and Kegan Paul, 1936).

2. Ibid., pp. 67, 171, passim.

3. Robert K. Merton, *Social Theory and Social Structure* (Chicago: Free Press of Glencoe, 1957), pp. 489–508; Talcott Parsons, "An Approach to the Sociology of Knowledge," in *Transactions of the Fourth World Congress of Sociology* (Louvain: International Sociological Association, 1959), Vol. 4, pp. 29 ff.

4. Talcott Parsons, *The Structure of Social Action* (New York: McGraw-Hill, 1937) pp. 473–87.

5. Cited in Peter L. Berger and Thomas Luckmann, *The Social Construction of Reality: A Treatise in the Sociology of Knowledge* (Garden City, N.Y.: Doubleday and Co., 1966), p. 6.

6. Maurice Natanson, *Philosophy of the Social Sciences* (New York: Random House, 1963), pp. 183 ff.

7. Berger and Luckmann, *Social Construction of Reality*, p. 15.

8. Ibid., p. 18. For a provocative discussion of the strengths of the Chicago School, and especially of their anticipation of the importance of emic categories for contemporary cultural anthropology, see Heather P. Kurent, "Frances Donovan and the Chicago School" (Ph.D. dissertation, University of Maryland, 1982). Social scientists inspired by phenomenology, most notably ethnomethodologists, are sometimes referred to as "The New Chicagoans." See Julienne Ford, *Paradigms and Fairytales: An Introduction to the Science of Meanings* (London: Routledge and Kegan Paul, 1975), p. 157.

9. Berger and Luckmann, *Social Construction of Reality*, p. 65.

10. Ibid., p. 61.

11. Ibid., p. 49.

12. Ibid., p. 52.

13. Ibid., p. 132.

14. R. Gordon Kelly, *Mother Was a Lady: Self and Society in Selected American Children's Periodicals, 1865–1890* (Westport, Conn.: Greenwood Press, 1974), p. xiv.

15. George C. Herring, *America's Longest War: The United States and Vietnam, 1950–1975* (New York: John Wiley and Sons, 1979), p. 281.

16. For a further refinement of Berger's theoretical position along the lines of more mainstream sociological analyses see James T. Borhek and Richard F. Curtis, *A Sociology of Belief* (New York: John Wiley and Sons, 1975).

17. C. Wright Mills, "Two Styles of Research in Current Social Studies," *Philosophy of Science* 20 (1953): 265–75.

18. Berger and Luckmann, *Social Construction of Reality*, p. 18.

19. Ibid., p. 81.

20. Ibid., p. 188.

21. Borhek and Curtis, *Sociology of Belief*, p. ix.

22. Northrop Frye, *Fables of Identity: Studies in Poetic Mythology* (New York: Harcourt, Brace, and World, 1963), p. 11.

23. E. D. Hirsch, *The Aims of Interpretation* (Chicago: University of Chicago Press, 1976), p. 139.

24. Clifford Geertz, "Blurred Genres: The Refiguration of Social Thought," *The American Scholar* 49 (Spring 1980), pp. 165–79.

25. This is overstated to emphasize a point. This assertion should be tempered to take into account the difference between a work of *fiction* and *fictional discourse*. As John R. Searle explains, "in the case of realistic or naturalistic fiction, the author will refer to real places and events intermingling these references with the fictional references, thus making it possible to treat the fictional story as an exten-

sion of our existing knowledge. The author will establish with the
reader a set of understandings about how far the horizontal conven-
tions of fiction break vertical connections of serious speech."

Searle concludes that "a work of fiction need not consist entirely
of, and in general will not consist entirely of, fictional discourse." See
John R. Searle, "The Logical Status of Fictional Discourse," *New Literary History* 6 (1975): 319–32. The fiction included in this study is
restricted to expressly realistic modes. (Note, for example, James
Webb's disclaimer in *Fields of Fire* that "while all the characters involved are wholly fictional, the fuel of this fiction was, of course, actual experience.") We hope thereby to isolate as evidence what Searle
terms "serious illocutionary intentions conveyed by pretended illo-
cutions."

Searle's position enables us to treat of some literary materials by
employing two criteria which we believe unobjectionable in the present context: 1) avowedly realistic narratives which 2) demonstrate a
high degree of intersubjective agreement. In view of the extensive
literature the fact/fiction issue has spawned in contemporary philosophy, Searle's position may be regarded as epistemologically moder-
ate. He attempts to steer between two conflicting traditions within
semantic philosophy: the picture theory of language (early Wittgenstein) and the game theory of language (later Wittgenstein). These
two positions have been argued most forcefully by Keith Donellan and
Richard Rorty, respectively. Donellan, the arch-positivist, denies in-
tentionality and subscribes to a rigidly "physicalist" view of reference. Rorty, the arch-pragmatist, holds that the very notion of correspondence to (a non-linguistic) reality is opaque and a chimera. For
a fuller discussion, see Keith Donellan, "Speaking of Nothing," *Philosophical Review* 83 (1974); and Richard Rorty, "Is There a Problem
about Fictional Discourse?" in *The Consequences of Pragmatism*
(Minneapolis: Minnesota University Press, 1982), Chapter 7.

While Donellan's position strikes us as hopelessly stringent, Rorty's seems far too permissive. Our purpose is to impugn the common-
sense notion of the fact/fiction polarity without obliterating it entirely. Searle's "speech-act" theory appears as the least counter-
intuitive candidate upon which to base a criterion for adjudicating
reliability in narratives. In sum, the "degree of constructedness" of
an interpretation *does* concern us to the extent that we have tried to
soften, and at the same time preserve, a problematic distinction between "war stories" in the two senses outlined by Searle.

26. William Westmoreland, *A Soldier Reports* (Garden City, N.Y.:
Doubleday and Co., 1976). Criticism of this memoir is found in Her-

ring, *America's Longest War*, p. 282. The cognitive commitments of the general officers who served in Vietnam are the subject of Douglas Kinnard, *The War Managers* (Hanover, N.H.: University Press of New England, 1977).

27. Clifford Geertz, *The Interpretation of Cultures* (New York: Basic Books, 1973), pp. 30–53.

2

Initiation

A lot of things had to be unlearned before you could learn
anything at all, and even after you knew better you
couldn't avoid the ways in which things got mixed.
—*Dispatches*, p. 210

Any past war seems to be psychological preparation for
the next one as the heroism and sacrifice shown in the
previous war is glorified and approved. This is achieved
by the way history is taught, by processions or celebra-
tions of peace-war anniversaries, by the building of monuments and war memorials, and the giving and proudly
wearing of medals and decorations. . . . Such behavior
betrays social values.
—*War: The Anthropology of Armed Aggression*, p. 189

So, as always seems to be the case . . . we were trained
by the wrong war.
—*A Rumor of War*, p. 34

In order fully to comprehend the ways in which meaning was
compromised and subverted *in* Vietnam, it is necessary first
to understand the range of meanings Americans brought *to*
Vietnam and how those meanings were constructed, maintained, and transmitted. Beliefs, values, ideas, concepts, categories, *meanings*—everyday knowledge in the broad sense in
which that term is employed in the sociology of knowledge

discussed above—must be taught and learned in and through institutions. "Because culture is learned," says Gordon Kelly, "the processes and terms in which it is conveyed are particularly revealing to the historian interested in reconstructing a group's world view."[1] The process of acquiring the culturally appropriate meanings of warfare and of defining the individual's rights and duties with respect to it is part of all societies which practice armed conflict.[2]

Americans who served in Vietnam went to war with very specific kinds of knowledge garnered from a variety of sources. In this portion of the study, it is our purpose to examine the kind of knowledge Americans had, insofar as it is possible to reconstruct it, and how they came to hold it. Although the Vietnam War narrators make no systematic effort to specify every enculturating agency's distinctive role in socializing members with respect to warfare, from their testimony recurrent patterns emerge. Most of the narrators insist that their images of war were molded by certain social institutions and take pains to identify these institutions and to appraise their influence. Sometimes offhandedly, but more often with a precise and analytic dispassion, the narrators endeavor to discern and convey the social forces that equipped them to comprehend war in the misleading ways they did.

Three agencies emerge as the dominant influences on a generation of Americans born immediately after the Second World War. These agencies—the media, the family, and the military—assumed the burden of socializing young males to fashion images of warfare. The images inculcated by these three agencies of enculturation proved remarkably consistent with each other and therefore mutually legitimating.

The single most significant characteristic of these Americans' initiation into "war-consciousness" is that warfare was presented in terms wholly inappropriate to the conflict in which they would actually participate. The three agencies veterans later identified as instrumental in "teaching war" accomplished that task by relying almost solely on World War II as the paradigm of modern war.[3] The media, the family, and the U.S. military all conspired by initiating these soldiers-to-be into thinking of war—*any war anywhere*—as a replication of "The Big One . . . WWII."

Although the conflict in Vietnam bore virtually no resemblance to that war through which Americans came to understand warfare generally, the agencies of initiation designated as such by the soldiers persisted in presenting that particular paradigm throughout the course of the fighting in Asia. It is, as the narratives record, cruelly ironic that the Vietnam War combatants' most pressing business upon arrival in the war zone was shedding the cultural knowledge they had accumulated about war. In order to cope, the soldiers had to make a cognitive transition between the categories derived from WWII with which they came equipped and those it was necessary for them to adopt in their new situation. For many—too many—such a transition proved impossible. They ended up casualties not so much of enemy mines as of American minds, lethal weapons when they cue the wrong responses in a world offering no second chances. One correspondent, likening the war to a school where failure was final, said, "we were all studying the same thing and if you got killed you couldn't graduate" (*D*, p. 224). To realize the extent and impact of this indoctrination into World War II mythology, it is necessary to analyze those agencies in and through which the process of initiation was accomplished.

The "John Wayne Wet Dream"

> We didn't have no flame-throwers. I didn't see no tanks in Saigon. They didn't have things like you see in the movies about WWII. It surprised me. I was expecting for the tank to come up there and do the John Wayne type of thing.
>
> —*Nam*, p. 83

> I told him that nothing was going to happen to me and he gave my shoulder a tender menacing pat and said, "This

ain't the fucking movies over here, you know." I laughed
again and said that I knew, but he knew that I didn't.
                                    —*Dispatches*, p. 22

More than any other single factor cited in the Vietnam War
literature, the media (especially motion pictures) served to
initiate young American males into the mysteries of making
war, the purposes that war is intended to accomplish, and the
role one is expected to adopt within that war. The references
to various media and media-spawned personalities as forging
images and ideas of what war is "all about" are ubiquitous. As
we shall witness, the information conveyed in those images and
ideas corresponds to a very different reality from the one that
would claim so many victims in Indochina. The terrible irony
echoed throughout the Vietnam War narratives is that Americans were prepared for waging a war that in the 1960s only
existed on celluloid, videotape, and in print. The American
fighting man of that decade was culturally geared to participate in a war that took its coordinates—tactical, psychological, and moral—from the conflict in Western Europe twenty-
five years earlier. The movies fed a generation a consistent diet
of war images from which Americans might learn to interpret
the nature of armed conflict. The most frequently cited films
are those portraying combat in WWII in terms of a global
struggle against a clearly identifiable evil which could only be
subdued by superior force. As such, WWII combat films became an important socializing influence, giving symbolic form
to a number of ideas which thereupon achieved the status of
everyday knowledge.

This WWII symbolism had particularly perverse consequences in the case of the Vietnam War. Because the ideas
concerning warfare mediated by the film industry could not be
empirically tested against direct experience, the average ten-
or twelve-year-old viewer was especially vulnerable to them.
This fact is acknowledged by the narrators attempting to
identify the sources of their knowledge and gauge their impact. Says one, "I'd seen a lot of war pictures growing up . . .
it's a confusion of a whole value system, thinking that the world
was one way, living on one set of rules. It's a rude awakening

to find that it was done on another set. . . . Everything is symbolism" (*EWH*, p. 97). It is these symbols, within which were "stored" meanings generated by the movies and consumed by the Vietnam warriors, that require elucidation.

The soldiers view the movies' ability to shape their perspective, and hence their behavior, as crucial to understanding their subsequent activity. Whether eliciting simple reflex sorts of responses or inculcating tremendously subtle sorts of cognitive processes, the movies played a crucial role in fostering beliefs. As an example of the former, the movie-as-Army-recruiter-surrogate, one soldier says, "With all my terror of going into the Army . . . there was something seductive about it. I was seduced by WWII and John Wayne movies" (*N*, p. 33). It is, however, the latter—the less overt sorts of viewer responses— which most forcefully attests to the movies' power to organize perceptions into a coherent belief system.[4]

Perhaps the most remarkable aspect of this enculturating efficacy is the movies' capacity to provide a cinematic frame of reference for structuring experience.[5] Apart from considerations of the actual content of the genre with which we will be concerned, the movies encouraged the audience to dissociate and depersonalize experience, to view life *as a movie*. This tendency to detach oneself from the ongoing flow of events in the perceptual field is a behavioral trait which movie-going made possible. The Vietnam War was, at least for some of the soldiers who fought it, *The Vietnam War Movie*, replete with a cast of characters that miraculously included them: "It was as though we were in an open-air theatre, watching a war movie" (*RW*, p. 67). This distancing technique could be horrifying in its implications: "I loved to just sit in the ditch and watch people die. As bad as that sounds, I just liked to *watch* no matter what happened, sitting back with my home-made cup of hot chocolate. It was like a big movie" (*N*, p. 93). Such a confession might be considered anomalous were it not reiterated, in varying formulations, throughout the narrative accounts offered by the soldiers.

For at least one perceptive correspondent, familiar with combat troops, this phenomenon came to hold a particular fascination. What he referred to as the "life-as-movie, war-as-

war-movie, war-as-life process" (*D*, p. 65) became one distin-
guishing characteristic of the Vietnam warrior. These warriors were taught by the media that experience was to be ob-
jectified and cast in terms of viewer and viewed. That is, not
only were the soldiers' particular perceptions symbolically
mediated by the movies, but also ways in which to perceive
more generally. As the reporter observed, "I keep thinking about
all the kids who got wiped out by seventeen years of war movies before coming to Vietnam to get wiped out for good. You
don't know what a media freak is until you've seen the way a
few of those grunts would run around during a fight . . . they
were actually making war movies in their heads" (*D*, p. 209).
Even though the reporter could recognize that Vietnam "was
not a movie" (*D*, p. 46), many of the soldiers continued to perceive it as such. As the radical discontinuity between the World
War II movies they had seen and *The Vietnam War Movie* they
were living came to be appreciated, the reviews the latter received became steadily more unfavorable: "One day at the
battalion aid station in Hue a Marine with minor shrapnel
wounds in his legs was waiting to get on a helicopter . . . and
a couple of sniper rounds snapped across the airstrip, forcing
us to move behind some sandbagging. 'I hate this movie,' he
said" (*D*, p. 188).

This voyeur mentality worked in often complicated and subtle ways to deprive experience of its immediacy. Certainly the
most debilitating effect of the "war-as-movie" view is the pa-
ralysis of imagination it fostered in confronting the reality of
death. While watching events occur at one remove from reality, the soldiers found it problematic to conceive of a world operating according to ironclad laws of causality, mortality among
them. As one commentator remarked, "We'd all seen too many
movies, stayed too long in Television City, years of media glut
had made certain connections difficult" (*D*, p. 209). Vietnam was
simply not a place in which "the characters get smacked around
and electrocuted and dropped from heights, flattened out and
frizzed black and broken like a dish, then up again and whole
and back in the game" (*D*, p. 46). Such movie-fed notions of
immortality almost never allowed for the possibility of the
hero—oneself, of course—dying. For many, that possibility as-

serted itself as a complete revelation: "For the first time the reality of where I was and where I was going slapped me back worse than a bad nightmare. Now I'm in the war. Oh, God, I could really die out here. Up until this point I never took it seriously. It was happening but it wasn't real. It was TV—hey, heroes and shit. No, I could really die in this fucking place. I wasn't ready for that. It grabbed me and shook me every way but loose" (*N*, p. 74). Their perception of war as a movie in which death is inconceivable speaks to the enormous power of the electronic visual media in providing the socializing forms in which knowledge is organized.

Of course, the movies provided not only a framework for perceiving war but also a cluster of significant symbols for interpreting it. If war was a movie, it was a particular kind of movie, containing recognizable elements. These elements served to reinforce war as a meaningful human activity pursued for specific ends. In the film genre universally cited in the narratives as instrumental in molding conceptions of modern warfare—WWII combat films—one figure stands out as the locus of symbolic significance: John Wayne. A close examination of the accounts growing out of the Vietnam War reveals several hundred direct references to the influence of the late actor, all of them affirming Wayne as the embodiment of the American warrior and therefore as the spirit of war itself.[6] In his films, Wayne served a crucial symbolic function: initiating young men into an understanding of war through the depiction of certain actions and the attitudes they dramatize.

To illuminate the pervasive influence of Wayne's screen image (and its comic-book analogue, Sgt. Rock) is to reveal culturally constituted assumptions about human nature that are so fundamental they belong to what Alfred Schutz called "the world taken-for-granted."[7] That is, they constitute that body of cultural knowledge most often affirmed by implication because such "facts" are so obvious there is no need to speak of them. It is only when the taken-for-granted world ceases to operate predictably (as in Vietnam) that these assumptions demand and receive conscious recognition and appraisal.

An example from John Wayne's cinematic repertoire of symbolic action will serve to illustrate this point. First and

foremost, Wayne signified heroism in his role as exemplary
warrior in World War II combat films.[8] That heroism was held
up as genuine, admirable, and replicable. Typically, Wayne's
heroism in these films consisted of acting aggressively under
fire without regard for personal safety. In taking the initiative, forcing a confrontation, overcoming obstacles—"kicking
ass" in the vernacular—Wayne gave concrete form to the abstract notion of heroism.[9] It was taken for granted by American soldiers that heroism was available to them in Vietnam
in the same way that it was to Wayne onscreen: displaying
aggression under dangerous conditions. Such behaviors and the
conditions under which they were triggered, however common
to the set-piece battles of World War II, were hopelessly unsuited to the grim realities of counterinsurgency warfare in
Indochina.

The fighting in Vietnam tended to render this WWII heroism unattainable. As a result, it lost its "taken for granted"
status and was ultimately discredited altogether. Because
Wayne's quintessential heroism proved simply lethal in Vietnam, soldiers would say, "Don't go looking for booby-traps, don't
go trying to be a hero, because all you are going to do is get
killed. And nobody gives a damn once you die" (*EWH*, p. 159).

The point here is not so much the fate of this particular notion (in the next chapter meaning-inversion is precisely at issue) but the ways in which members of a society uncritically
accept assumptions like "heroism equals aggression." This John
Wayne stance, what one commentator referred to as "the John
Wayne Wet Dream" (*D*, p. 20) because of its essentially ado-
lescent character, was one such assumption.

This "John Wayne Wet Dream" emanates from a fundamental conviction about reality. This core assumption holds that
the application of unremitting energy sustained by an indom-
itable will shall prevail. Thus we wage "wars" on crime, pov-
erty, drug abuse, cancer, on Communism (of which Vietnam
is one glaring example), littering, drunk driving, and so forth
in the belief that anything can be "conquered." That is, reality
is pliable provided we "assault" it with the appropriate material resources: time, money, technical expertise.

The best description of the world view erected upon this assumption is that offered by Peter Berger. Berger identifies an "engineering mentality" which is a strategic component of modern consciousness as shaped by the technological revolution of the recent past. He says:

> The main features of this engineering mind-set can be described without too much difficulty: an atomistic or componential approach to reality—the world is perceived as consisting of units that can be taken apart and put together again. Means and ends can be readily separated. There is a strong tendency toward abstract and preferably quantitative thinking. There is an attitude of problem solving or "tinkering;" any problem encountered is viewed as, in principle, soluble if only the proper technical procedures are to be found.[10]

Precisely such a congeries of beliefs proved instrumental in producing the debacle of the Vietnam War. For both the Pentagon policy-maker and the lowly PFC, it was an article of faith that renewed efforts to eradicate unwanted phenomena would ultimately succeed. Communism in Asia proved to be one among many such phenomena that discredited the basic presuppositions of this "engineering mentality."

To return to the preparation of young American males to fight a war, it is only necessary to understand that the "John Wayne Wet Dream" had a powerful hold on the minds of these boys. The simplest response to the image evoked by Wayne is the boy-as-hero fantasy: "I had flash images of John Wayne films with me as the hero" (*N*, p. 40). Such imagery quickly succumbed to a much more menacing reality than the one depicted in the movies. In fact, a soldier in Vietnam might disparage his comrades by identifying the cause of some unnecessarily heavy losses as the "John Wayne Wet Dream": "I think it's because they had some concept of that's the way it was done," said one trooper. "They watched too many John Wayne movies. It just wasn't that way" (*EWH*, p. 202). An exasperated sergeant is even reported to have told some careless troops, "There are two ways to do anything—the right way and the John Wayne way."[11] From all accounts, it appears that part of the soldiers' struggle in Vietnam included shedding notions with which their initiation-by-cinema equipped them.

Says one, "The thought crosses my mind that if this were a John Wayne movie, we could cut our way through with machetes or knives," and then bitterly adds, "It's a long way from Hollywood" (*TNL*, p. 24).

If the movies, via John Wayne, fed the Vietnam warriors a steady diet of heroism that might have proved possible in WWII, Vietnam made those images appear sterile and useless. One Marine tells how "I wanted the sort of thing I had seen in 'Guadalcanal Diary' and 'Retreat, Hell' and a score of other movies," but finds that the Vietnam War furnished no such opportunity for heroic drama: "Like the Marines in WWII newsreels we had charged up the beach and were met, not by machine guns and shells, but by the mayor of Danang" (*RW*, pp. 14, 50).

The most disconcerting and dangerous aspect of the "John Wayne Wet Dream" is that it was frequently granted the status of official military policy. The military encouraged American combat troops to muster an intransigent will expressed in uncompromising ferocity as the most effective strategy. Such a strategy sought to unleash the spirit of heroism on an enemy who was virtually invisible, over impenetrable terrain, in a brutalizing climate that played host to a type of warfare demanding stealth, surprise, and evasion. To invoke such an ideal was worse than foolish. It was fatal. And yet it was done—repeatedly. Commanders whose own combat experience was limited to WWII continuously mistook the nature of the Vietnam conflict. While it may have been sound tactics to "storm a beach" or "charge an emplacement" during "the Big One," in the sweltering heat of a triple canopy jungle such pugnacity was sheer folly. In the mountainous Central Highlands, these Blitzkrieg maneuvers invited destruction from snipers, booby traps, heatstroke, snakebite, or even (imagine this in war-torn France) man-eating Bengal tigers.

Of all the U. S. Armed Services, it was the Marine Corps that embraced the "John Wayne Wet Dream" and accorded it privileged status as battle strategy. In the spirit of Iwo Jima, Marines were taught that "the offensive is the only tactic worthy of the name" and that "the essence of the offensive was the frontal assault" (*RW*, p. 15). A more inappropriate method of waging a counter-guerilla war could hardly be imagined. During the siege of Khe Sanh, the most famous "battle" of the entire war, over 200 Marines were killed by enemy artillery because the troops were not ordered to dig adequate fortifications. "Digging is not the Marine way," announced General Cushman, commanding officer of I Corps. The Marine Command was so attached to their WWII role as assault troops that one correspondent observed that "Marines defending are like antichrists at Vespers" and later, out in the field with the leathernecks, concluded that "If this had been an Army operation we would have been digging now, correspondents too, but the Marines didn't do that, their training taught them more about fatal gesture than it did about survival" (D, pp. 105, 189). In fact, upon first landing in Vietnam in 1965, the Marines "were taught the rudiments of defensive warfare . . . but only in tones of contempt" because "the brigade C.G. [Commanding General] felt that bunkers destroyed a marine's 'offensive spirit' " (RW, pp. 15, 50). The very notion of "frontal assault, that quintessential Marine maneuver" and the romance it conjured up of "a line of determined men firing short bursts from the hip as they advanced on the enemy at a stately walk" (RW, pp. 15, 109) was a direct legacy of that "Paradigm War" so thoroughly dissimilar to the one in which it was now being employed.

Besides heroism, other fundamental assumptions about warfare were shaped by the movies in terms acquired from the Second World War. Most notably, assumptions about Good and Evil and especially the inevitability of American combat involvement in the service of the former are indicated in the narratives as constituting an integral part of initiation. In the movies in which John Wayne portrays the war hero, the aggression unleashed as overt violence is legitimated by the end it is designed to serve.[12] Wayne performs in the heroic mode to defeat Fascism—Evil Incarnate—in those WWII epics. The absolute wickedness of the enemy sanctifies massive bloodletting. (In the marginally cited genres—cops/robbers and cowboys/Indians—equally definitive forces of evil are annihilated: lawlessness and savagery). Wayne thus serves as an embodiment of the moral position that "there was nothing we could not do because we were Americans, and for the same reason whatever we did was right" (*RW*, p. 66).

All of the narrators treated in this study underwent initiation during the Cold War hysteria of the early 1950s when the Communist had succeeded the Nazi as the personification of Absolute Evil. As a pervasive cultural agency of initiation, the WWII movies served to enforce a mentality that identified evil with simple political labels. This mentality easily assimilated the substitution of hammer and sickle for swastika. Communism, like Nazism, was presented as monolithic and intrinsically evil—what theologians would label *malum in se*, evil by reason of its existence. As one narrator recounts, "but the truth is that M [Company] didn't need to know its enemy to abominate him, just as it didn't need Thomist philosophy to appreciate that God is good. Communism's wickedness seemed to M to be sewn into the primeval warp of the universe, it was indelible like the earth's magnetic field, it was axiomatic: for M had never yet in its twenty years of life heard otherwise" (*M*, p. 131).

This pre-defined equivalence of Communism with Evil, coupled with the characteristic means for confronting evil depicted in films—eradicating it through violence—led Americans to understand their enemy as "the bad guys" who deserved destruction at the hands of "the good guys"—the Americans themselves. This belief was a model of clarity and parsimony: Communists were evil; therefore, killing them was necessary and good. Hadn't that, after all, been the central lesson imparted by John Wayne in all those films of heroism? As one soldier put it, "You see the baddies and the goodies on television and at the movies. I wanted to get the bad guy. I wasn't a patriot. I didn't join for the country. I could've given a fuck for this country then. I wanted to kill the bad guy" (*N*, p. 241). Movie-fed notions of morality that neatly divided the domain of humans into ethically polar opposites and prescribed the necessary punishment for falling into the wrong category were an important part of the belief-system Americans took overseas along with their duty bags.

Like the idea of heroism, the belief in Americans' intrinsic goodness *vs.* Communists' natural wickedness fared miserably once it encountered the reality of the Vietnam War. As one combatant ruefully recalls, Americans transported "along with our packs and rifles the implicit convictions that the Vietcong would be quickly beaten and that we were doing something altogether noble and good. We kept the packs and rifles; the convictions we lost" (*RW*, p. xiv). Another testifies that "what really bothered me were some of the things that I saw that were not compatible with the ideals that I'd been brought up to believe in, in terms of being a member of the military and fighting for a country that heroically helped defeat the Germans and the Japanese and was supposed to be the good guy and all of that" (*EWH*, p. 68). Exactly what this soldier and his comrades-in-arms "saw" in Vietnam will be the subject of the following chapter, but, clearly, it was not what he had been initiated to believe he would find. In the words of one, "The Second World War was very impressive to a child; it was also a kind of entertainment, and they painted Vietnam in the same style. It took some of the teeth out of it. It put Vietnam under the same moral umbrella as World War II" (*WL*, p. 11).

Perhaps the most curious (and spurious) notion associated with media-molded morality concerning warfare is *fair play*, an idea which seemed consistently to elude the grasp of the Vietcong. In the WWII combat movies, fighting takes place according to certain largely unstipulated, yet nevertheless clear and binding, rules. Like a sport or game, warfare is a performance given by participants of varying levels of accomplishment whose success or failure depends upon the application of those skills within carefully circumscribed limits. In refusing to honor those regulations, the code that makes the game possible, one denigrates the pursuit altogether. Americans espoused these notions and, tragically, applied them wholesale to the war in Vietnam. One soldier admits, "I tended to look upon war as an outdoor sport, and the shelling seemed, well, unfair" (*RW*, p. 110). Another simply "spoke of the war as if it were a wild, good-natured kind of poker game as so many others have" (*WL*, p. 297).

Again, the idea of fair play met a quick and violent end in Vietnam when the absence of rules, especially those presented as integral to combat in WWII, became immediately

apparent. Referring to a VC offensive during which saboteurs
sneaked into an American compound to dynamite a hospital,
one soldier mused, "TV taught me there's a right way and a
wrong way to go out and kill somebody. I imbibed that shit
from my childhood on . . . the firefights I had out in the field,
I can rationalize that for myself. You say, they knew the risk
as well as you did. It was a fair fight" (*N*, p. 170). Another remembers, "I saw things that weren't right. Maybe this isn't
Sgt. Rock after all . . . I felt something was really wrong here"
(*N*, p. 254).

The soldiers' own role within this deceptively simple axio-
logical system was constructed almost entirely out of trans-
planted WWII expectations. This role, and the quasi-religious
imagery in which it is couched, is apparent from even a cur-
sory viewing of the films that constitute this genre. These films
depict the Allied soldiers as welcome liberators of an enslaved
civilian populace, as harbingers of freedom and hope, and as
providers of security and moral authority before which the
forces of tyranny recede. In short, the American GI is por-
trayed as embodying a singularly redemptive impulse. Moreover, the GI is to be recognized as such by the soon-to-be-
redeemed populace. Embraced and kissed by grateful women,
cheered by elated men, and idolized by awed children, the
flower-bedecked GI could instantly understand his cause and
his country as just and his service to them noble. As one Vietnam warrior observes, "We expected them to run out and welcome us like the World War II type of thing. 'Hey, GI. Yay,
you the Americans' " (*N*, p. 212). This sentimental and idealized portrait reflects the initiation-by-cinema of large numbers
of Americans. They were certain that their reception by an indigenous population in any land where they came as self-ap-
pointed "rescuers" would include gratitude because they, after
all, were "the good guys."

Indeed, a close examination of the Vietnam War narratives
reveals that the dominant image to which Americans automatically appealed was that of *saviors*. This role was one they
had been socialized to adopt, and, like so much else, it fell apart
in Vietnam. One soldier ruefully recounts, "We are supposed
to be saving these people and obviously we are not looked upon

as saviors here . . . if we came into a village, there was no flag waving, nobody running out to throw flowers at us, no pretty young girls coming out to give us kisses as we march through victorious" (N, p. 189). The GI's steadily growing disappointment over the failure of certain members of the cast in *The Vietnam War Movie* faithfully to play their parts is a chink in the edifice of good guy/bad guy morality. Acting convincingly in the role of savior presumes a reciprocal response on the part of the "saved." Such a display was, however, conspicuously absent. The soldiers' appraisal of their reception by the Vietnamese is revealing. One soldier reports the natives as conveying the sentiment, "Oh, here come the fucking Americans again. Jesus, when are they going to learn?" (N, p. 189). This dashing of expectations becomes central to establishing the collapse of meaning in Vietnam.

As stipulated, this savior role demanded suitable victims in need of saving to recognize their plight. The classic victims of war are the elderly, women, and children—those presumed most helpless and defenseless. It was these people, stereotyped in countless WWII films, whom the Americans expected to be most appreciative. In Vietnam, it was precisely these prototypical victims who were most leery of the large, American intruders. As one would-be savior comments, "We were told that we were going to help the people and defend them and protect them from Communism and people trying to take away their land, and that people really liked us because we were, you know, we were like their—saviors. And when we got there, the people sort of, you know, they looked at us funny, and the children would run when we came" (CWA, p. 99). Initiated to think of themselves as saviors, unequivocally good and moral beings acting to preserve the freedom of a proud people, Americans ended up as characters in an unintelligible movie for which they had no adequate preparation: "I was told we were going to save the Vietnamese from the Communists. We didn't save anyone. We just killed. Why were we sent there? I can't honestly say" (CWA, p. 55).

Besides providing definitions of heroism and structuring conceptions of morality, the media also helped to construct an overwhelmingly powerful concept of manhood and masculin-

ity. Like heroism, the idea of manhood bears a special relationship to participation in war. For the hero, war is a natural
environment, an arena in which the human energies that define him can receive their fullest play. The opportunity to exhibit heroism outside of warfare, although possible, is unlikely. Even in combat, the circumstances favoring an outburst
of heroic action are infrequent. In short, heroism isn't available to all men. Its emergence always hinges on an unpredictable confluence of events and personalities. The dreamlike
quality in the John Wayne Wet Dream is precisely the constant, controlled, and repeatable nature of the violent energies unleashed—their frequency and duration.

Manhood, like heroism, finds its best area of application and
display in war. Unlike heroism, however, it relies on much more
accessible human energies for definition. In the narratives,
manhood and masculinity are equated with overcoming ad-
versity, a kind of diluted, quiet heroism. Being a "man" consists of demonstrating endurance. This ability to prevail in the
face of hardship, discomfort, fear, and pain, to be durable and
resilient, is an index of masculinity. Americans were so thoroughly initiated that "after fifteen years of it, it was in-
grained. It was the fight that mattered, not the cause. It was
the endurance that was important, the will to face certain loss,
unknown dangers, unpredictable fates" (*FF*, p. 33). War is the
obvious and logical testing ground for manhood thus conceived. It is in a war that the chances to try one's powers of
steadfastness are most often and most unambiguously found.

Most commonly, war is understood as a test of the power to
achieve control over the primal anguish: fear. Before discovering even physical pain, the individual confronts and must
cope with the feeling of terror. A male who subdues or at least
separates himself from the fearful being inside earns the social identity "a man." The opposite of a man in this usage is
not a woman but a coward, a degraded form of humanity relinquishing the rights and privileges of the male gender while
qualifying for none of those conferred upon the other. A coward is genderless, a social condition analogous to the political
position of being stateless—without a place to occupy in the
human family.

Ideally at least, a man can pass the test of war by showing fearlessness. This process entails not only refusing to acknowledge fear but also never experiencing it: " . . . and M [Company] wasn't afraid. Experience had anesthetized it to these sounds of battle during its winter of Army training, its many years of John Wayne" (*M*, p. 87). At the very least, one must be "man enough" to submit to the test so that one's measure can be accurately taken. As one soldier confessed, "I had another motive for volunteering, one that has pushed young men into armies ever since armies were invented: I needed to prove something—my courage, my toughness, my manhood, call it whatever you like" (*RW*, p. 6).

Because fear is a biological necessity for the human species,[13] this expectation could hardly be consistently met. However, the biological fact does not diminish the importance of cultural forms in regulating the organism's perception, interpretation, and reaction. There were (and are) appropriate cultural responses to the feeling of fear. Fear can be admitted, its intensity acknowledged, and its urgings confessed, but in the world of visible human activity it must be granted no causal efficacy. Thus, manliness requires not only that one disavow, but also determinedly ignore, the promptings of the terrified being inside. "Fear was taboo. It could be mentioned, of course, but it had to be accompanied with a shrug and a grin and obvious resignation" (*IID*, p. 141). The recipe for manhood is thus "acting wisely when fear would have a man act otherwise. It is the endurance of the soul in spite of fear" (*IID*, p. 137).

The power of this conception of manly endurance to shape behavior is one that we would find remarkable were it uncovered in an exotic culture by Western anthropologists. It is, literally, more important to retain one's manhood than one's life because the latter would be socially worthless without the former. One paratrooper recalls:

In jump school any number of people were scared shitless, but they jumped—because they were told over and over that everybody was just as scared, but a "man" jumps anyway. The idea being that if they followed their instincts and didn't jump, they just weren't men. So they jumped—because the thought of quitting and losing their manhood was worse than the thought of being splattered over the drop zone (*TNL*, p. 70).

Clearly the possession of the characteristics that qualify one for membership in the fraternity of men (in this instance airborne wings) are dearer than life. As the jump school graduate concludes, "the fear that makes us go back again and again is stronger than our fear of dying or death: it's the fear of losing our manhood" (*TNL*, p. 70).

The idea that one submits to the tests of manhood by going to war and acquitting oneself according to this cultural code is repeated through the narratives. War is the ultimate test of the capacity to endure not just fear but also any form of travail from minor irritation to imminent death and disfigurement. Moreover, one is not only required to submit to hardship but also actively to seek it in order that certification be made: "I wanted to go to war. It was a test I wanted to pass. It was a manhood test, no question about it . . . I led a pretty unchallenged life. I didn't know where I was going, so I might as well detour for a while and come up against something that was really hard" (*N*, p. 52). For all the popular sentiment which regards young Americans who did not experience the Great Depression as somehow "soft," the Vietnam literature gives the lie to the belief that this was their choice. For so many, it was necessary to go to war in Southeast Asia to disown their heritage of affluence: "Having known nothing but security, comfort, and peace, I hungered for danger, challenges, and violence" (*RW*, p. 5). The motivation is so often sadly recognized as "the old beliefs about war: It's horrible, but it's a crucible of men and events and in the end, it makes more of a man out of you" (*IID*, p. 31).

As a proving ground for this kind of endurance, Vietnam offered ample opportunity to display "manhood." War, in this view, had been romanticized for Americans into a kind of "placement test," the results of which determined who would wear the social identity of "man" and who would be stigmatized by the label "coward."[14] War was thus a kind of diagnostic tool for uncovering human "essences" that might otherwise

remain forever concealed. Thus, war as an instrument designed to reveal the truth underneath mere appearances was
a notion dramatized by the media: "Plus I had read all the war
fiction . . . it implanted this idea in my mind that war was a
place for you to discover things" (*N*, p. 27). Perhaps the final
word on endurance belongs not to a Vietnam warrior but to
another sort of culturally defined "man" from another age altogether—Socrates: "But what would you say of a foolish endurance? Is not that, on the other hand, to be regarded as evil
and hurtful?"[15]

Brief Excursus: The Green Beret

In the Special Forces A camp at Me Phuc Tay there was
a sign that read, "If you kill for money you're a mercenary. If you kill for pleasure you're a sadist. If you kill for
both you're a Green Beret."

—*Dispatches*, p. 257

Our argument thus far was intended to show how war movies
helped shape a particular generation's conception of war and
especially how they molded that conception in terms of a previous war which bore virtually no resemblance to the one waged
in Vietnam. Most of the references in the soldiers' accounts are
to these movies, several to that medium still relatively new
when Vietnam warriors were growing up—TV—and only a
handful to the printed word. We contend that the efficacy of
the visual media as a socializing agency for initiating Americans cannot be overestimated. Indeed, since concepts such as
heroism, morality, and manhood are, if not invented, at least
repeated and socially maintained with a high degree of symbolic consistency by the media, it would be impossible to understand American culture without acknowledging the functions it performs.[16] By presenting certain behaviors as
meaningful, the media distributes culture every time a human encounters one of its offerings. In some instances more

than in others, it is apparent that the media is the creator, rather than a passive reflector, of a cultural phenomenon. The Green Berets are a case in point.

Thanks almost entirely to the mass media, the United States Army Special Forces—the Green Berets—came to occupy a prominent place in American war mythology. In that lore, the soldiers who served in Special Forces and wore its distinctive headgear were the embodiment of precisely the social values we have analyzed: heroism, morality, manliness. They were presented by the media as pure distillates of the human traits that constitute these lofty abstractions: ferocity, goodness, fearlessness. As such, they served as a powerful symbol for generating traditional (WWII) meanings about the nature of the Vietnam War in which their exploits first received public attention.

Ironically, the U. S. Special Forces were created, trained, and equipped expressly to fight World War III, had their image fashioned after the U. S. Army Rangers of World War II, and saw action only in the Vietnam War. Few Americans realize that Special Forces were formed in 1952, many years before their publicity breakthrough, in accordance with Cold War thinking about the nature of the next global conflict. At that time, policy makers believed that any future war would take place in Europe as the result of Soviet invasion through Germany. Special Forces' mission was to parachute in behind the advancing Soviet columns in order to organize, train, equip, and lead insurgents, relying always on the support of the people to overthrow their Russian oppressors. In sum, Special Forces were to operate as guerillas, just as did the VC in South Vietnam. They were never designed to function as a *counter*-insurgency unit because in principle such a force's chances of success were slim.[17] Counterinsurgency was, however, precisely the role to which they were assigned in Vietnam.

In keeping with the spirit of their original mission, fighting an unconventional war against an unpopular government by mobilizing partisans, the Special Forces' homework included a reading list of the classics: Mao, Che, Tito, Ho. Quartered in a semi-secret staging area, the U. S. Special Warfare Center at Fort Bragg, the Special Forces trained diligently for a dozen

years for a Soviet attack that never came. In fact, the Green
Berets were anything but a "hot property" during their form-
ative years. Until 1961, when President Kennedy visited their
home in North Carolina, the Special Forces were a poor relative of the 82nd Airborne Division. They were known (when
they were known at all) as "Sneaky Petes" because they usually had to scrounge for supplies. At that stage in their career,
the Department of the Army considered them not so much elite
as useless in the day-to-day functioning of the organization.
(Indeed, their most marketable and distinctive symbol, the
beret, had been outlawed years before. The Army had clamped
down on the wearing of non-regulation issue because it de-
plored the idea of "private armies.")[18]

All of this changed with the President's visit. With the massive media coverage garnered routinely by the Office of the
Presidency, the Special Forces were immediately hyped as
"Kennedy's Own." On the verge of being swallowed up by the
U. S. Army Rangers, the Green Berets suddenly enjoyed enormous publicity and attention. Almost immediately, the beret
was reinstituted by Presidential order, the understaffed Special Forces began processing applications in record numbers,
and funds were allocated for a newer, larger Special Warfare
Center that would become the showpiece of the Army. By the
time teams were readied to tour the country demonstrating
their skills, the Green Berets had become media darlings. As
the Regular Army types joked about their suddenly famous
cousins in their distinctive dozen-man units, "How many people in a Special Forces' A Team?" "Twelve. Eleven Green Berets and a cameraman."

As the media recognized that the Green Berets were indeed
capturing the imagination of the American people, the Special
Forces mania reached fever pitch. In 1965, the Green Berets
were honored by a number 1 pop song, a number 1 best-sell-
ing book, and a full-length, high-budget motion picture star-
ring (but of course) John Wayne. Within a year, there was
Green Beret bubble gum, Green Beret toy weapons, a Green
Beret exercise book, Green Beret dolls, etc. As one team leader,
who had joined the Sneaky Petes when they were still a cloak-
and-dagger secret weapon, remarked, "So successful was the

PR campaign that it not only survived the death of its biggest booster, John F. Kennedy, and the interservice resentment of the 'regulars,' but actually continued to grow. We weren't a hard product to sell and the American public was ready" (*TNL*, pp. 198–99).

The story of the Wayne movie *The Green Berets* is especially revealing in this context. Even more than the book, which one cynic described as "the only recruiting pamphlet to make the best-seller list," Wayne's film presented the Green Berets in blood and guts terms borrowed entirely from WWII Commando activities. Because the Green Berets' actual mission, "reconnaisance, surveillance, and training,"[19] was hardly the stuff of action drama, Wayne substituted more familiar fare: a classic "behind-the-lines" kidnapping of a high-ranking Viet Cong officer and a pitched battle against the enemy attempting to overrun the beleaguered defenders of a U. S. camp. The sensitive nature and complex politics of the actual role the Special Forces A Teams played in Vietnam were nowhere to be found. That role, for example, often involved living among the Montagnards and exploiting their thousand-year-old hatred for the ethnic Vietnamese. Indeed, Special Forces A camps were usually little more than mercenary compounds, the dozen Green Berets acting as paymasters for "the Yards" with CIA funds. Wayne, however, depicted the Green Berets as a latter-day "Dirty Dozen," carrying out suicide missions against impossible odds in an effort to help out the freedom-loving South Vietnamese.[20] As one commentator suggested, "the movie wasn't really about Vietnam, it was about Santa Monica" (*D*, p. 188).

The media thus manipulated public opinion and shaped public sentiment to view these soldiers and, by extension, the war in which they were engaged as noble, glamorous, and necessary. The Green Berets were the living embodiment of the John Wayne Wet Dream. The emphasis on the romantic aspects of that dream obscured the reality of a war that would not conform to what one soldier recognized as "our Hollywood fantasies" (*RW*, p. 15):

And the movies. They were their own communion. If John Wayne wasn't God then he was at least a prophet . . . a half-dozen friends would walk the five miles into Hillsville on Saturday afternoons and sit in awe through *The Sands of Iwo Jima, The Bridges at Toko-Ri, The Guns of Navarone, Anzio, The Battle of the Bulge*, and dozens of others. It was all there on the screen. Standing up and fighting back (*FF*, p. 34).

Unfortunately, Vietnam may have been "like you are in your own movie . . . but you certainly ain't John Wayne" (*N*, p. 101), who may well be responsible for more combat casualties in Vietnam than any other American, civilian or military.

Fathers and Sons

> We bought dented relics of our fathers' history, rusted canteens and olive-scented, scarred helmet liners. Then we were our fathers taking on the Japs and Krauts along the shores of Lake Okabena, on the flat fairways of the golf course, I rubbed my fingers across my father's war decorations, stole a tiny battle star off one of them and carried it in my pocket.
>
> —*If I Die in a Combat Zone*, p. 20

> First letter I got from my old man was all about how proud he was that I'm here and how we have this duty to, you know, I don't fucking know, whatever . . . and it really made me feel great. Shit, my father hardly said good morning to me before. Well, I been here eight months now, and when I get home I'm gonna have all I can do to keep from killing that cocksucker. . . .
>
> —*Dispatches*, p. 29

If the movies (and to a lesser extent television, comic books, and popular fiction) proved to be a powerful influence in determining a conception of warfare rooted in the particular realities of WWII, the various media were nonetheless distant and disembodied, a one-way conduit of information. In contrast, face-to-face interaction, especially with those George Herbert Mead designated "significant others," can have an even more telling effect on the formation of cultural knowledge.

These "consociates,"[21] as some social scientists refer to them, exert direct influence by transmitting and legitimating beliefs about reality. As discussed in the introduction, the sub-discipline of the sociology of knowledge explains how such knowledge comes to be held by investigating the processes constituting social interaction. It is primarily through such face-to-face social interaction, in the course of what Peter Berger calls "conversation" in an extended and specialized sense, that our fundamental conceptions of reality are constructed and maintained. "It is in conversation, in the broadest sense of that word, that we build up and keep our view of the world going . . . we all exist within a variety of social networks or conversational fabrics which are related in often complex and contradictory ways with our various conceptions of the universe."[22]

Socialization of novices into a particular world view, what we have referred to as initiation, is accomplished in and through "conversation" in this sense. Moreover, it is principally in conversation with significant others that interaction achieves its reality-shaping efficacy. Where the "conversational fabric" is of a very close weave, i.e., where the individual is most deeply committed to and implicated in the ongoing communication and its consequences, he is most likely uncritically to accept as given the assumptions about reality imbedded in the discourse. Again, it is these assumptions about reality that make up the "normal," "natural," "commonplace," "everyday" world—the *taken-for-granted* world of the phenomenologist Alfred Schutz. Where the "conversational fabric" is sufficiently loose, the assumptions may be regarded as not entirely self-evident, problematic, or even doubtful, i.e., their certainty is diminished to the level of probability or mere opinion. Instances of a social network that admits of a loose weave of conversational fabric might include strangers chatting on a train, hagglers in a market, or patients in a waiting room at a hospital. The premier example of a social network in which the conversational fabric is tightly woven, i.e., consisting in "persons having such relations more or less continuously and to some enduring purpose, rather than merely sporadically or incidentally,"[23] is the family.

The family, at least in America, is the primary socializing

agency within which children receive their basic orientation to the reality they inhabit. "To become a parent is to take on the role of world-builder and world-protector . . . parents provide the environment in which a child's socialization takes place and serve as mediators of the entire world of the particular society in question."[24] Because "cultural continuity requires not simply that a group's beliefs be explained to the young or to initiates, but that the validity and importance of those beliefs be successfully justified to, and internalized by, those who will eventually be responsible themselves for maintaining the belief system,"[25] the family assumes a tremendous burden with particularly weighty consequences.

If socialization is successful, the belief system or world view is transmitted intact, and other socializing agencies within the culture—educational, religious, and economic institutions, among others—will serve to confirm that world view or at least important aspects of it. Because the family matrix is one locus of social process where face-to-face interaction is constant and regarded as vital by all participants, and where, due to the dependent condition of its charges, reward and punishment can be administered swiftly with predictable results, the family's opportunities for effectively socializing the child and ensuring cultural continuity are extraordinary.

The soldiers' war stories attest to the remarkable power of the family as a world-builder, an arbiter of meanings, particularly meanings attached to the activity of making war. The Vietnam narrators identify their culturally mediated conceptions of war as being generated literally by "conversation" (oral transmission). In virtually every instance, the responsibility for explaining and justifying the necessity of war devolved upon close male kin, predominantly the father. Typically, fathers (and occasionally older cousins, uncles, or grandfathers) were those who had already gone to war and having returned could therefore provide the succeeding generation with the vital, presumably accurate information required to prepare themselves for making war.

In the case of the Vietnam narrators, the fathers had, in nearly every case, served in WWII, and the conversation about war was conducted exclusively in terms engendered by that conflict. War, so the fathers recounted and the movies bore dramatic witness, was an activity ordered on the model of the Second World War. It was a stage on which heroism could be displayed, an arena for the struggle between Good and Evil in which American forces always acted to ensure the triumph of the former, a testing ground in which manhood could be proved by enduring suffering with equanimity. In this respect, the social mechanisms for "teaching war" were operating smoothly insofar as they (the media and the family) were mutually affirming and reiterating notions about war coherently and consistently.

In particular, fathers invoked the ideal of manliness and presented war as the breeding ground for this estimable trait. Because heroism was unpredictable and goodness taken for granted as intrinsic, manhood, in the sense discussed above, was impressed upon the young as a desirable consequence of participation in war. Indeed, manhood could only finally be verified in combat, and thus war was more than just another activity; it was a basic rite-of-passage from boy to man. For that reason, many American fathers gladly sent their sons to the war in Vietnam and encouraged them to enlist. One dutiful son recalls, "My old man, when the war came, he says, 'Oh, go, you'll learn something. You'll grow up to be a man. Go.' Shit, if my folks had to send their little poodle, they would have cried more tears over that than over me. But I'm supposed to go because I'm a man" (*N*, p. 35).

This dual sense of war as simultaneously forging manhood and providing optimum conditions for its emergence is one that harks back to the fathers' own experience in WWII. Their meaning system was produced by social circumstances which included their role as victors in a moral crusade against dictatorship, their transformation from boys into men through participation in that crusade, and the solemn duty they assumed of changing the shape of history by defeating America's enemies. One Vietnam warrior remarks, "I grew out of one war and into another . . . I was the offspring of the great campaign against the tyrants of the 1940s . . . I was fed by the spoils of 1945 victory" (*IID*, p. 20). The fathers invariably taught their sons to view the Vietnam War as a chance, an

opportunity not to be missed, an experience designed to rep-
licate the epic grandeur of their own coming-of-age: "Well, my
father of course was pleased as punch. He wanted to see me
go . . . He thought that would shape me up, make a man out
of me. He was a sergeant in the big one, so he was looking
forward to me trying to . . . There was really no conception
of the war" (*EWH*, p. 102). One could readily argue that even
had the fathers had a "conception of the war"—known that it
was wrong or unwinnable or unnecessary—their response
would still have been the same. Manhood requires only that
one demonstrate endurance as its own end, not in the service
of some larger political or moral goal. Recounted one soldier,
"My father wrote that at least his son was discovering how
much he could take and still go on" (*IID*, p. 139).

But the fathers provided something more than simply en-
couragement to attain manhood, powerful though that was. The
fathers also offered a justification for going to war that tran-
scended the individual son's fate, that dwarfed the concern with
taking one's measure, and that overrode the imperative to prove
oneself for one's own gratification. In what sociologists of
knowledge refer to as a "strategy of legitimation," the fathers
initiated the sons into a trans-personal idea of duty involving
obligation, honor, and historical continuity. This strategy made
willingness to go to war a matter of moral debt rather than
personal volition.

In a way in which the media simply wasn't capable of doing,
the fathers taught their sons that war was to be understood
as an opportunity, even a privilege, to discharge a debt owed
not to themselves, or even to the fathers directly, but to the
past, to heritage and tradition. As it is reported in the Vietnam narratives, this complex, confusing, and contradictory
notion is the single most powerful factor, what anthropologists of war designate the "releasing stimulus," disposing the
Vietnam veterans to join in that conflict. To understand this
idea of duty to the past, i.e., to one's culture and one's prede-
cessors, is to confront the tremendous power the family exercises in formulating meanings which organize behavior. That
a young man still in his teens would volunteer to risk his life
in a war that he might find morally dubious (many soldiers

truly thought we "had no business there") because of an obligation to "individuals who do not even share a community of time and so, by definition, cannot interact"[26] with him, tells us a great deal about the fathers' influence over their progeny.

To comprehend fully the notion of duty to the past, it is necessary to extricate it from its residence in particular family milieux which vary considerably (although we shall return it there shortly) so that we might look at it schematically. The abstracted components of the idea of "duty" look roughly like this: since they first set foot in the New World, the people of America have had to engage in bloody conflicts to ensure their survival. (The wars against the original Americans, the Indians, would be an example.) These wars crop up periodically—approximately every generation. Each generation has answered the call to arms, fought successfully, and guaranteed biological survival and hence cultural continuity. In order that this continuity be preserved, it is necessary for each generation to form an unbroken chain with the preceding one, upholding the same meanings by attaching them to the same activities. Cultural continuity thus demands an *uninterrupted succession* of willing warriors who fight because it has always been done. As prior generations have laid down their lives in sacrifice, so must present and future ones. The original motive for engaging in war—group survival—is no longer a prerequisite. Simply that wars were fought now becomes sufficient reason for wars to continue being fought. It is thus to the past—variously designated tradition, heritage, culture, civilization, the "American way," or what have you—that the most fundamental allegiance is owed. A simple syllogism clarifies the logic of this meaning system: if duty equals debt, and debt avoided equals disgrace, then debt repaid equals honor. An even sharper formulation comes from the narratives which indict "patriotic ideas about duty, honor, and sacrifice, the myths with which old men send young men off to get killed or maimed" (*RW*, p. xvi).

Like so many other notions that were killed-in-action in Vietnam, this one proved easy enough to internalize: "I learned about the Second World War, hearing it from men in front of the courthouse, from those who had fought it. The talk was tough. Nothing to do with causes or reason; the war was right, they muttered, and it had to be fought" (*IID*, p. 21); "I had an uncle who told me what the fighting had been like on Iwo Jima, an older cousin who had fought with Patton in France and who could hardly talk about the things he had seen" (*RW*, p. 76); "One way or another in every generation when there was a war, some male in the family on my father's side went to it. I never had it drilled into me, but there was a lot of attention paid to the past, a lot of not-so-subtle 'This is what a man does with his life' stuff when I was growing up. I had been, as we all were, victimized by a romantic, truly uninformed view of war" (*N*, p. 33).

Obviously, reinforcing the notion of duty to the past was simplified because the past that was invoked did not reside in a sterile museum or musty archives, but was a living past that had touched the individual's life directly in the form of his own father and perhaps father's father: "I had also been kind of brainwashed since I was a kid. My father had been a Marine in the South Pacific during WWII. Although he never talked about it all that much, when I was in the 2nd grade I had his web belt and his Marine Corps insignia" (*N*, p. 29); "We went into the Marine Corps with the same feeling our fathers and grandfathers had gone into the service. There wasn't anybody around to tell us that we hadn't done the right thing. And then to find out later that all those people had died in vain" (*EWH*, p. 29).

It is this recognition that people can "die in vain" in a war waged by Americans that was the death knell for the notion of duty to the past.[27] If the fighting can even once be recognized as futile or meaningless, a destruction of tradition rather than an upholding of it, then "that one continuous linking that had bound father to son" (*FF*, p. 33) disintegrates. The soldiers whose initiation placed heaviest emphasis on this notion are characteristically those most vehement in exposing it as fraudulent in light of their Vietnam experiences: "I was over there until I was late 19, early 20 years old. I volunteered you know. Ever since the American Revolution my family had people in all the different wars, and that was always the thing—

when your country needs you, you go. You don't ask a lot of
questions, because the country's always right. This time it didn't
turn out that way" (*EWH*, p. 50). The realization that many
were drawn to Vietnam on the assumption that it was right
to fight because Americans before had fought, forced them to
question the nature of the particular fight in which they were
embroiled. As we shall see in the next chapter, the concrete
circumstances of the Vietnam War cancelled any debt they
might have felt they owed.

This issue of transmitting a set of assumptions about war
across generations in order to establish cultural continuity,
what we have called "fathers and sons," is most thoroughly
explored in one particular text in the Vietnam canon, *Fields
of Fire*. James Webb, an Annapolis graduate who served with
the Marines in Vietnam, devotes considerable attention to the
act of going to war as a bond that unites generations. Webb's
alter-ego in the novel, Robert E. Lee Hodges, perceives the
fulfillment of his destiny as going to war and thus consum-
mating "that one continuous linking that had bound father to
son" (*FF*, p. 33). It is precisely how Hodges comes to hold this
view of his fate that Webb illuminates so clearly and dramatizes so effectively. For it is "the front-porch chronicles of . . .
who had fought and fallen" that provide Hodges his perspective (*FF*, p. 29).

Specifically, Hodges is taught family history, the chronicle
of unabated bloodshed which is the stuff of his past. From the
war with the Cherokee to the battles fought by his most immediate forebears, he learns he has "an inherited right to violence." His grandfather "who breathed the gas for Pershing"
is linked to him as is his father who fought "knee-deep in the
snow at the Battle of the Bulge." The importance of his past
is that "it was a continuum" primarily because of war, and it
is his duty to keep it intact (*FF*, pp. 29–32).

Hodges, like so many American GI's, has no special desire
to fight the Vietcong. "He was not anxious to save Vietnam
from itself and he did not relish facing North Vietnamese guns
for a year, but he reasoned that, after all, a man cannot choose
his country's enemy. Had Grandpa really hated the Hun in
1917, until told he should? And besides, Vietnam was some-

thing to be done with, a duty" (*FF*, p. 35). Within the framework of Hodges' biography, Webb explores the notion of duty
and identifies it as a social mechanism for enforcing cultural
continuity, an ideational cement that bonds each generation
of males by redeeming them in the eyes of the preceding ones.
The result of honorably discharging one's duty is "that same
emotion passing with the blood: a fierce resoluteness that . . .
came to accept the fight as birthright" (*FF*, p. 33).

What Lt. Hodges comes to realize is that "if there had been
no Vietnam, he would have had to invent one . . . but there
was Vietnam, and so there would be honor. It was the fight,
not the cause that mattered" (*FF*, p. 34). Hodges fulfills his
destiny by fighting in Vietnam. After several months in the
bush, he is offered a comfortable job in Okinawa as a recreation officer but declines the safety of the rear for the honor of
the war zone. He is killed, like his own father, "in a town he
could not pronounce, much less spell" on the fields of fire. Un-
beknownst to Hodges, he has fathered a son while taking R&R
in Okinawa. The son, inquiring after the father, is told that
he had been a brave warrior who died gloriously for a noble
cause. The son determines that he, too, will be a soldier and a
credit to his father's memory.

Webb's vision of fathers and sons is profound and definitive.
It is a detailed exploration of the psychological and social processes by which the notions of duty and honor are legitimated
in American culture. As a strategy for initiating individuals
into full adulthood, the "offering of oneself on the altar of one's
culture" (*FF*, p. 31) is the ultimate rite-of-passage. Webb dem-
onstrates how generation after generation of fathers and sons
enact this cultural dance of going to war to keep faith with
the past. In Hodges' words, "I fight because we have always
fought. It doesn't matter who" (*FF*, p. 25).

Fathers taught sons the nature of war using their own experiences in WWII as a model. By levying on the notions of
manhood and duty outlined above, the fathers presented war
as a blessed event. Had the Vietnam War proved itself amenable to the world view of the fathers, those notions would have
survived intact to be re-transmitted by the sons to future initiates. As we shall see, however, the Vietnam experience was

not one from which the idea of duty and its corollaries—obligation, honor, continuity—would emerge unscathed. Rather, Vietnam made a whole generation of fathers look like liars and betrayers, and a whole generation of sons victims of their own initiation.

Praying for War

> We had a prayer on the wall. All the Marine barracks in Parris Island have this prayer. It's a prayer for war. Every night before we went to bed at nine o'clock we had to pray that there'd be a war, so that the Marine Corps could always be on the move, because that was their job, to fight.
> —*Conversations with Americans*, p. 38

> To understand what happens among the mine fields of My Lai, you must understand Fort Lewis Washington. You must understand a thing called basic training.
> —*If I Die in a Combat Zone*, p. 40

If a particular perspective on reality (a world view, belief system, or meaning system) is to retain its plausibility, then the "conversation" that produces and maintains that perspective must be conducted in a suitable social setting. A suitable social surround will, usually by implication, confirm the assertions about the world that constitute the system. Clearly, some social settings are better geared to the construction of distinctive realities than are others. For instance, the so-called scientific outlook which characterizes the present age in the industrialized West exists only because its plausibility is maintained in and through social process.[28] We are taught science and live among its technological by-products. Without the taken-for-granted "miracle" of electricity and all the other routine "miracles" of everyday experience to provide verification of and reinforcement for that world view, the world view itself totters and collapses.

Anthropologists doing fieldwork in remote lands among exotic peoples find that without the mundane and commonplace appurtenances upon which a scientific outlook rests, the urge to "go native"—to shed one's own world view in favor of the indigenous majority's—can be almost irresistible. Even in contemporary America, the presence of diverse sub-cultures embracing alien meaning systems, what Peter Berger calls "cognitive minorities,"[29] makes "going native" a possibility here and now. One journalist, writing in the mid–1960s about out-law motorcycle gangs in California, reported that after a year of drinking and riding with the hoodlums he found himself "no longer sure whether I was doing research on them or slowly being absorbed by them."[30] The point, quite simply, is that "human thought is consummately social: social in its origins, social in its functions, social in its forms, social in its applications."[31]

This characteristic of human consciousness has enormous consequences. We have seen, for instance, how particular en-culturating agencies can mold a distinctive world view which generates socially appropriate behavior. The family distributes meanings to its younger members in such a way that those meanings are accepted uncritically, at least until an experience like the Vietnam War poses substantive threat to those received meanings. As a "conversational network," the family commands sufficient time and attention to make socialization a relatively efficient process. However, with respect to the initiate's time and attention, even the family does not have a monopoly.

The family must compete with other conversational networks which offer complementary, but also conflicting, world views. The initiate, that is, is subjected to a variety of networks whose world-building power varies considerably. This fact of pluralism—the availability of more than one world view—makes initiation, at least by the family, a somewhat more challenging task than was previously suggested. Because our views "will depend upon the continuity and consistency of such conversation," they "will change as we change conversation partners."[32] This means, inevitably, that the conversation partner who receives the fullest hearing (by either "drowning out" other discourse or isolating the initiate from it) is most likely to prove authoritative.

There is at least one social institution that can and does offer sufficient isolation from, and therefore effective negation
of, competing world views: the military. In American society,
at least, the military (especially during that explicitly initia-
tory phase called basic training) provides the individual with
a wholly circumscribed social universe whose parameters are
clearly drawn with gates, barbed wire, and armed guards.
Within the confines of the military post during this period, the
"trainee" or "recruit" has no access to any "conversation" except that designed for his consumption by the institution. Deprived of any alternative sources of meaning, the trainee almost invariably adopts the frame of reference defined by his
social context. He "goes native" in the very real sense of shedding a civilian world view and adjusting to the new meaning
system demanded of him: soldier.

The military thus serves as a "total institution,"[33] in the
words of Erving Goffman. Like the prison or the mental hospital, the military is empowered to function with maximum
efficacy and ruthlessness as a re-socializing agency. It is
equipped with the means (including instruments of violence)
to impose a world view without regard for the rights or modes
of legal redress that society normally grants its adult members. The military assumes complete control over, and responsibility for, the recruit, dictating even the performance of the
most fundamental instinctual behaviors—eating, sleeping, de-
fecating—and harshly punishing deviation from its rules. To
paraphrase Berger on the issue of initiation into a world view
in which pluralism poses no obstacle to reality-construction: it
is easy to be a soldier in a social situation where one can limit
one's significant others to soldiers, where one in fact has no
choice in the matter, and where all the social forces are geared
to support and confirm a soldierly world view.[34]

Of the three social institutions identified in the narratives
as conveying conceptions of war along particular (and particularly inapplicable) lines, the military receives the most bitter
condemnation. The narrators view the military as the final
stage of their initiation into war, a finishing school that gives
concrete form to notions first encountered through the media
and the family. The military's failure to modify those notions

to accord with the unique reality of Vietnam is thus considered the monumental betrayal. Put bluntly, the military is accused of sending boys off to fight and die in a war for which they had inadequate preparation. Ideology, they insist, was substituted for information, and therefore the true nature of the conflict took them by surprise.

In every instance where the military is specifically designated as the cultural agency molding meanings of warfare, the unique power of a total institution is dramatized. Thus to speak of the military as a separate society is accurate because trainees were initiated into a new cosmic order:

The Marine Corps, as we quickly learned, was more than a branch of the armed services. It was a society unto itself, demanding total commitment to its doctrines and values, rather like one of those quasi-religious military orders of ancient times. . . . We were novitiates, and the rigorous training, administered by high priests called drill instructors, was to be our ordeal of initiation (*RW*, p. 8).

This "other society," which stands apart from the conventional meanings and symbols of civilian life, existed only to fulfill its single function: waging war. As one soldier notes, "The subject is separated from his normal references, that is, his social environment" in order that he master the fundamentals of "good citizenship" in this society: "to kill effectively, efficiently, and on command" (*TNL*, pp. 99, 97).

This ability of the total institution absolutely to invert meanings attached to particular behaviors is crucial to the fashioning of its end product: a trained killer. For most Americans, taught very early that life is sacred, such a systematic inversion of meaning is only possible in a total institution. In a total institution the notion of the sanctity of life can be continuously drained of meaning:* "You run around in the morning singing 'Airborne Ranger.' Every time your left foot hits the ground they yell 'Kill, Kill!' When you get through, you're

---

*The idea of tenderness receives similar treatment because it is incompatible with the "cold-bloodedness" required to kill: "There is nothing named love in the world. Women are dinks. Women are villains. They are creatures akin to Communists and yellow-skinned people and hippies" (*IID*, p. 52).

breathing fire. It's just drilled into you" (*EWH*, p. 100); "And
when we had to go and eat we went to the mess hall and we
had to yell 'kill' at the top of our lungs three times before we
were allowed to eat" (*CWA*, p. 138). This process of substituting a military cosmos glorifying the taking of life for a civilian
one of revering it, what we have called "praying for war," is
one that has far-reaching implications for the initiate. As one
NCO recalls, "The process of changing a man into a soldier is
brutalizing even if he never kills another" because "the individual seldom recognizes his own brutalization, his changing
sense of values . . . basic training does many things to men.
Nobody remains unchanged by it" (*TNL*, pp. 96, 248). As we
shall see, the profound consequences of basic training became
most apparent in Vietnam.

This process of teaching a recruit to "pray for war" is neither terribly complicated nor mysterious. Once the individual
is stripped of normal referents, virtually any reality that is
sufficiently stable, predictable, and coercible—in a word, intelligible—will be embraced in the face of massive uncertainty. The basic training regimen exploits this basic sociological fact by implementing the necessary confusion and
furnishing its antidote: a system of meaning that restores shape
and coherence to the world. After having been "stripped of all
past supports" by being made to "run from one strange environment to another to perform unfamiliar tasks . . . he is
prepared to start 'living by the book,' thereby becoming a soldier" (*TNL*, pp. 100, 101). This change from civilian to soldier
is simply an application of the kinds of insights routinely generated by the sociology of knowledge for explaining any "community of faith" as a "constructed entity"[35] subject to manipulation and modification.

Such manipulation affects not only specific perceptions, but
(as we saw in the case of film) the mode of perceiving itself:
"A year earlier, I would have seen the rolling Virginia countryside through the eyes of an English-major who enjoyed
reading the Romantic poets. Now I had the clearer, more
pragmatic vision of an infantry officer. Landscape was no longer
scenery to me, it was *terrain*, and I judged it for tactical rather
than aesthetic value" (*RW*, p. 21). Through concerted manip-

ulation of the parameters of meaning, especially by repetition, new meanings are produced and legitimated: "In time he begins to believe that he really does love the Marine Corps, that it is invincible, and that there is nothing improper in praying for war, the event in which the Corps periodically has justified its existence" (*RW*, p. 12).

Once the social order of the military has disestablished previous meanings attached to human morality (and given the recruit the skills to exploit it and the motive for doing so), the military must provide the appropriate object on which to train such a world view. And it is this, more than any other aspect of military training, that arouses the wrath of the Vietnam narrators. During the dozen years of the Vietnam War, soldiers were taught to focus their murderous impulses not on a faceless "enemy" as they would during peacetime, but on an entire race: the Oriental. "We had bayonet training in boot camp everyday. We had to scream 'kill' when we stuck the bayonet into the dummy. Then we had to beat the dummy up, hit it with a rifle butt and stick the bayonet into it. And we had to call the dummies a dirty mother-fucking gook, or slant-eye" (*CWA*, p. 33). It is this central facet of their initiation that the writers find most destructive of their dignity, most corrosive to their morality, and most necessary and powerful for explaining their actions in Vietnam. Soldiers in all branches of the armed services recount receiving essentially the same indoctrination. They learned not only how to kill, but who most richly deserved killing. Whether called gook, slant, slope, dink, Cong, Charlie, VC, Red, Commie, or a half-dozen local variations, the message was the same: the enemy is Oriental and inferior. Because the power to mold meanings and enforce their usage is so vast in a total institution, soldiers had few resources to resist such ideas, had they even aspired to do so. The idea of the "brotherhood of man" is no more resistant to social processes than is the "sanctity of life." Each idea survives or perishes by virtue of the social support it receives. In the military anyone who espoused either of these ideas was subjected to the same mechanisms of social control upon which civilian society relies to enforce compliance: therapy (in the broad sociological sense of practices designed to still doubts and prevent lapses of conviction), humiliation, and, ultimately, physical abuse.

The military enjoined its members to adopt one particular belief which resulted in tremendous excesses once transported to the battlefield: the Oriental was fundamentally different in kind from the American. The history of this notion obviously predates the first American involvement in Indochina in 1950. Yet, most of the plausibility of the idea (and within belief systems it is plausibility that matters) was of fairly recent vintage. Specifically, the soldiers were trained by NCO's, "lifers" as these career soldiers were called, who had already fought Oriental enemies and were thus in a position to affirm and confirm their "otherness." The vast majority of the initiators had seen action in WWII against the Japanese, in Korea against the Chinese and North Koreans, or, in many instances, *both*. The terms used to refer to the most recent Oriental enemy, the Vietnamese, had all been employed previously by Americans at war to designate the yellow-skinned peoples. Thus, Orientals of the several nationalities (some of whom are the bitterest of enemies themselves) were lumped together to blend into one "non-white other."

The American GI's were taught that the Vietnamese were different in kind and inferior as either sub-humans (a radically impoverished form of the species homo sapiens) or as non-human altogether (a lower animal or even inorganic material). In both instances, Americans attributed to Orientals the absence of fundamental human traits—emotion, reason, compassion, intellect, faith, and so forth. This perception of the Vietnamese as biologically and culturally degraded life-forms had predictable consequences: "If you convince your soldiers that the enemy is less than human, comparable to baggage at best, a child assassin at worst, and then inform them that their mission is to score high in the body count exercise, you cannot feign surprise when you discover what the war has become" (*CWA*, p. 13); "And throughout the training they emphasized the animalness of the Vietnamese. They were sub-human we were told. We could do anything we wanted to them when we got there. They told us you could kill this gook and then cut him apart. He wasn't human" (*CWA*, p. 36).

In the above quotations, the soldiers allude to two of the unique circumstances that made the Vietnam War so hideous. In no other war in which America has engaged has the body count (and its corollary, the kill ratio) been the sole measure of military effectiveness. The body count, quite simply the number of corpses each engagement with the enemy produced (and its logical entailment, the quantity of enemy dead relative to "friendly dead"), took the place of what had, in previous wars, been referred to as "strategic aims": taking land, capturing a force, breaking through enemy lines, threatening a capital city, etc. In a guerilla war, however, the only demonstrable success lay in stacking up bodies. "Addressing a group of marines, Greene had told them they had a single, simple mission to accomplish in the war: 'You men are here to kill VC'" (*RW*, p. 112). The emphasis on high body counts, coupled with the belief in the Vietnamese's innate inferiority, gave rise to the mentality expressed in the phrase "if it's dead and it's Vietnamese, it's VC" (*RW*, p. 69). The logic of the situation was particularly perverse because the troops were taught that "there aren't ten slopes worth even one GI" (*TNL*, p. 233). Therefore, the possibility of a "favorable kill ratio" was virtually nonexistent. It was the proverbial no-win situation because the lives that were being traded and counted in the muck of the rice paddies were held to be of fundamentally incommensurate worth. As one soldier commented, "No one in Alpha Company gave a damn about the causes or purposes of their war: It is about 'dinks and slopes' and the idea is simply to kill them or avoid them" (*IID*, p. 84). Tragically, the soldiers' training had taught them that killing "gooks" is of no more gravity than exterminating an animal: "We come across this old papa-san dying in the dirt in a hooch. Mama-san is there leaning over him. The dude walks up, pulls out that .45 and blows the fucker's brains out. Says to me, 'I was just helping the fucker out.' Then he turns around and shoots this mother and her baby. Steps outside the hooch and says, 'Snake'" (*N*, p. 196).

This kind of wanton slaughter is one of the most ghastly effects of the initiation of U. S. soldiers into a world view based on "just pure, simple racism" (*CWA*, p. 179). The issue of

atrocities committed by GI's (taken up in detail in the next
chapter) is one that cannot be understood apart from the
training they received, especially their instructors' insistence
on child assassins. The young, traditionally the most vulnerable and therefore best protected of non-combatants in war,
played a special role in the preparation of Americans to meet
the enemy in Vietnam. The constant emphasis on child assassins reveals a good deal about the strength of the conviction
in Vietnamese "otherness." For the Americans, as we have seen,
the Vietnamese weren't human and therefore neither were their
offspring. Instead, they were regarded as miniatures of miniatures—descendents of already non-human entities—not
subject to the moral rules which guide the conduct of civilized
beings.

Soldiers were repeatedly warned that Vietnamese youth
weren't children but a sort of human-looking piece of ordnance, all the more dangerous because of its deceptive pack-
aging: "We had classes about how the kids might have weapons or explosives hidden on them. That they might get near
us and kill us. They could be walking charges" (*CWA*, p. 194);
" 'Let's say you're on a trip to Saigon,' the sergeant had
squawked in his $10 public-address system voice . . . 'and a
cute little kid on a bicycle leans it against the wall. It may
blow up! Now in Saigon you can trust no one! No one; Man,
woman, or child!' " (*M*, pp. 112, 113). Praying for war meant
demonstrating a readiness to take life without regard for the
age, gender, or physical condition of the target, i.e., until the
last vestiges of civilian meaning had been completely undermined and erased: "Our DI was telling us that the one thing
that is really hard in the Marines is to get used to the idea of
little kids being killed because when they first get over there,
most of them are sympathetic to children. This is the way
Americans are brought up, plus the fact that a lot of Marines
have their own kids and everything, but they trained us to be-
ware of them." (*CWA*, p. 132).

If there seems to be one theme that unites the varying experiences of soldiers who were trained to serve in Vietnam, it
is this poisonous admixture of racism and paranoia. Praying

for war within the terms set by training in the U. S. military entailed having the desire to, and being proficient at, killing Orientals—"wasting gooks" as it was called. Taught that "women and even small children may carry weapons and charges, that all young men are to be regarded as suspects," the soldier soon comes to understand that "the enemy has been identified—he is everywhere, he is everyone" (*CWA*, p. 11). A "sensible" approach, therefore, encouraged a soldier to "trust in nothing that isn't already dead" (*VHD*, p. 43). As one laconic soul who had learned his lessons well put it, "I mean if we can't shoot these people, what the fuck are we doing here?" (*D*, p. 29).

Clearly, the soldiers' bitterness toward the military is fundamentally different in kind from the rancor they reserve for the media or their fathers. Whatever idealized or romantic images were proffered by those two influences, they tried to preserve a sense of human dignity and impute a sense of lofty purpose to the activity of making war. It was only the military, however, that simultaneously elevated war into an activity worthy of prayer and degraded the men who invoked the Deity to provide it. Taught as civilians "thou shalt not kill," then re-socialized into the most effective means of doing so, and supplied with an entire race of people on which to practice, the military condoned and even rewarded what the soldiers themselves designate as their own worst impulses: "You can begin to understand how genocide takes place . . . you can take anybody given the right circumstances and turn him into a wholesale killer. That's what I was" (*N*, p. 154); "You fuckers want me to kill . . . anything I can. Chickens, dogs, anything. . . . It's a shame I was so crazy" (*N*, p. 315). Perhaps the best observation on what men can be socialized to become was offered by one intelligence officer. Called upon to interrogate suspected Vietcong by the method jokingly referred to as "The Bell Telephone Hour" (attaching electrodes to the suspect's genitals and running the current from a field telephone through his body), he said, "The war took my measure. Not just me, but me and my culture. The culture had given me a frame-work, a point of reference for understanding myself, my religion, and my parents, my background and all . . . I was exposed as another barbarian along with the rest" (*N*, p. 215–16).

Advancing Toward Retreat

I wasn't dumb, but I sure was raw, certain connections are hard to make when you come from a place where they go around with war in their heads all the time.

—*Dispatches*, p. 21

We have investigated, from their own reports, how a particular generation of Americans "learned war." They did so by exposure to a variety of enculturating agencies which made armed aggression meaningful in terms of culturally constituted values. In a very real sense, Americans did "go around with war in their heads," and it was the purpose of this chapter to analyze both the kind of war they had in mind and the various social institutions through which that image of war was constructed, maintained, and transmitted. War, as should be obvious, is a matrix for meanings that are neither necessary nor stable. Heroism. Morality. Manhood. Duty. Honor. Tradition. Power. Superiority. These are the culturally relative meanings with which a generation of Americans—raised on WWII movies, Dad's WWII stories, and WWII-style military training—went off to fight the enemy. None of these meanings inhere ineluctably in the activity of warfare, although each does serve to motivate members of the society to take up arms. Had John Wayne been regarded as a suicidal fool, or Dad a senile anachronism, or one's drill instructor a homicidal psychopath, none of the meanings imputed to war would have proved sufficiently plausible to serve as the premises of behavior. It is necessary, therefore, to remember that social reality is "an ongoing human production"[36] open to modification on the basis of a fuller understanding of the consequences of our beliefs about it.

To appreciate fully the consequences of the soldiers' initiation, it is necessary to scrutinize the ways in which the meanings they held toppled like the proverbial dominos. Their dizzying descent into the chaos of the Vietnam vortex can be gauged by the extent to which instinct asserted itself to impose meaning when social institutions failed to. We shall, that is, reconstruct from the soldiers' accounts the world they inhabited in the war zone—where the only meaning resided in sheer survival.

NOTES

1. Gordon Kelly, "Literature and the Historian," *American Quarterly* 27 (Spring 1974): 141–59.

2. As Anthony F. C. Wallace succinctly states, "There are few, if any, societies that have not engaged in at least one war in the course of their known history, and some have been known to wage war continuously for generations at a stretch." See Anthony F. C. Wallace, "Psychological Preparations for War," in *War: The Anthropology of Armed Aggression*, eds. Morton Fried, Marvin Harris, and Robert Murphey (Garden City, N.Y.: The Natural History Press, 1968), p. 173.

3. The use of the term *paradigm* and all its derivations throughout this study should not be misconstrued as having any relation whatsoever to the hotly debated and idiosyncratic usage of the historian of science Thomas S. Kuhn. By stretching the meaning of *paradigm* to include some two dozen disparate concepts, Kuhn has rendered its use exceptionally risky. We mean the term as simply synonymous with "a model." For the best critique of Kuhn's erratic usage and especially his enormous impact outside of natural science, see Ian Hacking, review of Thomas S. Kuhn, *The Essential Tension*, in *History and Theory* 17 (1979). (A publication of Wesleyan University Press.)

4. For a fuller discussion of the influence of media in shaping viewers' conceptions of reality—what is generally called "audience theory" in mass communications research, see Paul F. Lazarsfeld and Robert K. Merton, "Mass Communication, Popular Taste, and Organized Social Action," in *Mass Culture: The Popular Arts in America*, eds. Bernard Rosenberg and David Manning White (New York: Van Nostrand Reinhold, 1957). For an additional overview of theories of media, see Michael R. Real, "Media Theory: Contributions to an Understanding of American Mass Communications," *American Quarterly* 32 (1980): 238–58.

5. See Lawrence Howard Suid, *Guts and Glory: Great American War Movies* (Menlo Park, Calif. Addison-Wesley, 1978), p. 102. Suid remarks that "For most Americans in recent years . . . the reality of life and the illusion of the screen are tightly intertwined."

6. Ibid., pp. 92–102. Suid notes that "not until John Wayne created the role of Sergeant Stryker in *Sands of Iwo Jima* and then merged his own personality with the character did Americans find a man who personified the ideal soldier, or Marine. . . . Wayne's military characterizations ultimately established him as America's quintessential fighting man. While this image has come to pervade American society to the extent of becoming a cliché, it remains a powerful influence on the nation's youth. Wayne, in fact, became the model of action for several generations of young males, representing the traditional American ideal of the anti-intellectual doer in contrast to the thinker."

7. Alfred Schutz, *The Problem of Social Reality:* Volume II of *Collected Papers* (The Hague: Nijhoff, 1962), pp. 17–19.

8. Lawrence Howard Suid, "The Film Industry and the Vietnam War" (Ph.D. dissertation, Case Western-Reserve, 1980), pp. 110–12.

9. Suid, *Guts and Glory*, p. 107.

10. Peter L. Berger and Hansfried Kellner, *Sociology Re-interpreted: An Essay on Method and Vocation* (Garden City, N.Y.: Anchor Books, 1981), p. 123.

11. Suid, *Guts and Glory*, p. 106.

12. Ibid.

13. J. Maynard Smith, "The Evolution of Alarm Calls," in *Readings in Sociobiology*, eds. T. H. Clutton Brock and Paul H. Harvey (San Francisco: W. H. Freeman and Co., 1978), p. 183.

14. For an illuminating discussion of the dynamics of identity formation and the hierarchical structure of socially available identities, see A. F. C. Wallace and R. D. Fogelson, "The Identity Struggle," in *Intensive Family Therapy*, eds. I. Boszormenyi-Nagy and J. Gramo (New York: Harper and Row, 1965). For a cross-cultural perspective, see John Caughey, "Personal Identity and Social Organization," *Ethos* 8 (1980).

15. Plato, *The Dialogues*, trans. Benjamin Jowett (Oxford: Clarendon Press, 1953), p. 68.

16. This function can best be designated "the production of culture" because it emphasizes the active role communications media take in determining, instead of passively reflecting, cultural reality. See Richard A. Peterson, *The Production of Culture* (Beverly Hills, Calif.: Sage, 1976).

17. The British example in South Africa, The Boer War, is especially instructive in this regard. In many ways, the fighting between the Boer guerillas and Her Majesty's forces prefigures the conflict between the V. C. guerillas and the U. S. regulars. For a detailed account of U. S. Special Forces' training for, and mission in, Vietnam, see Donald Duncan, *The New Legions* (New York: Random House, 1967), pp. 174–92.

18. After the Special Forces' publicity breakthrough in the early 1960s, berets proliferated throughout the U. S. Armed Services. Tank crews, helicopter crews, the Navy's River Patrol Force, and other units designated "elite" adopted the beret in a variety of colors.

19. Suid, "The Film Industry and the Vietnam War," p. 126.

20. Ibid., p. 137.

21. "Consociates" is a term employed by Clifford Geertz, borrowed from Alfred Schutz, to designate people who are "involved in one another's biography" and thus "grow old together." The term indicates a type of social relationship distinct from "contemporaries" on the one hand, and "successors" on the other. For a fuller discussion, see Clifford Geertz, *The Interpretation of Cultures* (New York: Basic Books, 1973), pp. 365–66.

22. Peter Berger, *A Rumor of Angels* (Garden City, N.Y.: Doubleday and Co., 1969), p. 34.

23. Geertz, *Interpretation of Cultures*, p. 365.

24. Berger, *A Rumor of Angels*, p. 154.

25. Kelly, "Literature and the Historian," p. 154.

26. Geertz, *Interpretation of Cultures*, p. 366.

27. The idea of owing those who had fought in the past included the most recent past—as recent as the day before. Our perpetual refusal to withdraw from Vietnam, even after it was apparent that eventually we must, was expressed in popular sentiment as reluctance to render the sacrifices of those who had already been killed there meaningless. If we withdrew, instead of pursuing our hopeless policy, they "will have died in vain." Of course to continue the war would inevitably result in more American casualties whose deaths would have to be similarly consecrated. This viciously circular reasoning was elevated to the level of official U. S. policy during the administration of Richard Nixon and dubbed "Peace with Honor." See George C. Herring, *America's Longest War: The United States and Vietnam, 1950–1975* (New York: John Wiley and Sons, 1979), pp. 164–70.

28. For a thorough analysis of the complexities of a distinctively modern outlook, one aspect of which is the reliance upon scientific

perspectives, see Peter Berger, Brigette Berger, and Hansfried Kellner, *The Homeless Mind* (New York: Vintage Books, 1973), pp. 23–41.

29. Berger, *A Rumor of Angels*, pp. 15–19.

30. Hunter S. Thompson, *Hell's Angels: The Strange and Terrible Saga of the Outlaw Motorcycle Gangs* (New York: Vintage Books, 1973), pp. 23–41.

31. Geertz, *Interpretation of Cultures*, p. 360.

32. Berger, *A Rumor of Angels*, p. 34.

33. Erving Goffman, *Asylums* (Garden City, N.Y.: Anchor Books, 1961), pp. 7–34.

34. Berger, *A Rumor of Angels*, p. 44. Berger uses the example of a Catholic in an orthodox social context to indicate the relative lack of obstacles to inculcating faith in a non-pluralistic environment.

35. Ibid., p. 38.

36. Peter L. Berger and Thomas Luckmann, *The Social Construction of Reality: A Treatise in the Sociology of Knowledge* (Garden City, N.Y.: Doubleday and Co., 1966), p. 198.

3

The Retreat from Meaning

It was like that lieutenant had told us back at the airstrip, "This is our world. You went to Hell and you're still
alive." I understood it.

—*Nam*, p. 85

I can't justify it. . . . That's it, you see. When meaning
becomes purely personal, so does glory. No great cause. It
makes less and less sense.

—*Fields of Fire*, p. 117

How far into this must we go to find meaning?

—*If I Die in a Combat Zone*, p. 169

The way I feel about Vietnam—I don't give a fuck about
North Vietnam or South Vietnam. Them mother-fuckers
can fight forever. I don't care as long as they don't fuck
with me, man.

—*Conversations with Americans*, p. 83

We have thus far sought to adumbrate the meanings a generation of American soldiers carried as cultural knowledge
about war. Those meanings were constructed and maintained
through the social support they received in the United States
(including U. S. military installations overseas) and functioned as part of the taken-for-granted world inhabited by the
GI. This world-taken-for-granted served as the cognitive

premises for the American combat soldier's behavior. Our purpose in the present chapter is to investigate the fate of those meanings once they were transported to the war zone and subjected to the very different conditions that obtained there.

To trace the fate of those meanings (and the soldiers who held them), it is necessary to bear in mind the most basic axiom of the sociology of knowledge: "Ideas do not succeed in history by virtue of their truth but of their relationship to specific social processes."[1] Our analysis of the socializing agencies responsible for initiation into war consciousness demonstrated the relationship between the GIs' ideas and the social processes through which they were constructed, maintained, and transmitted. That is, we saw how certain ideas could achieve the status of taken-for-granted knowledge in the everyday world of practical activity. It is now necessary to subject certain aspects of the world-taken-for-granted to further scrutiny. Specifically, we shall elaborate on the processes by which reality is socially constructed and, more importantly in the case of the Vietnam War, how that reality may be dismantled.

Sociologists of knowledge insist that "every human society rests on assumptions that, most of the time, are not only unchallenged but not even reflected upon. In other words in every society there are patterns of thought that most people accept without question as being of the very nature of things."[2] It is the sum of these unquestioned assumptions that forms the world-taken-for-granted. Such patterns of thought are open to enormous variation, both historically and across cultures. In every instance, though, these assumptions will serve the same crucial function. They furnish "the cognitive and normative tools for the construction of a coherent universe in which to live."[3] Because so much of everyday reality may be accepted as "given" by members of a particular society, those members can function effectively. By defining the boundaries of possibility, the taken-for-granted reality narrows the range of choices available to individuals. This fact enables human activity to assume social forms. In short, the world-taken-for-granted makes society possible.

A dialectical model of society in which theories and ideas

continually interact with the human activity from which they spring best accounts for the phenomenon of social forms. In the sociology of knowledge model, social worlds are produced by social activity and in turn act back upon that activity. Because "the socially produced world attains and retains the status of objective reality in the consciousness of its inhabitants in the course of common, continuing social activity . . . the status of objective reality will be lost if the common social activity that served as its infra-structure disintegrates."[4] Just as any world-taken-for-granted depends upon "reality-confirmation," so it is vulnerable to "reality disconfirmation." Put simply, all socially produced worlds require validating social experience.

Because a particular reality is "testable" in this sense, it is necessary to speak of any social world as "taken-for-granted until further notice."[5] Such a cumbersome phrase draws attention to the *precariousness of belief systems.* "Just because all human worlds are 'constructions,' " says Peter Berger, "so they are fragile, contingent and finally destined to be swept away."[6] In a world-taken-for-granted until further notice, "notice is sometimes given in a variety of ways—through an intensification of social conflicts, through economic or *military disasters*, through natural catastrophes or, more rarely, by means of religious or quasi-religious enthusiasm. In such situations, the basic structures of society become problematic. [emphasis added]"[7]

Instances of the disintegration of such taken-for-granted worlds abound. The scientific world view discussed earlier provides such an example. Most of the properties of man and nature thought to have been adequately accounted for by a religious world view in earlier times are now subsumed under scientific categories. Insofar as Western man automatically appeals to those categories as the only possible valid ones, it is proper to speak of the hegemony of the scientific outlook and the eclipse of the religious one. That is, the scientific framework now has the taken-for-granted status previously enjoyed by the largely discredited religious meaning system. What was obviously an instance of spirit possession to a typical citizen of seventeenth-century Salem appears to us to be a clear case of psychological or physiological aberration explicable by reference to scientific theories of pathology. Such ideas as "unconscious motivation" or "chemical imbalance" are plausible to us in a way that witches and demons no longer are.[8]

This precariousness of meaning systems can best be understood within the framework of the sociology of knowledge through two key concepts: objectivation and plausibility structures. These concepts explain the specifics of reality maintenance, the processes necessary to keep a view of reality going. Also, and most crucially, the concepts of objectivation and plausibility structure enable us to comprehend how a particular reality can collapse.

Objectivation "is a process by which subjectively experienced meanings become objective to the individual and, in interaction with others, become common property and thereby massively objective."[9] We witnessed, for instance, how the notion of manhood outlined in the previous chapter became objectivated to the extent that it was experienced as not only massively real but also of paramount value. Objectivations are maintained through plausibility structures, "a collection of people, procedures, and mental processes geared to the task of keeping a specific definition of reality going."[10] A plausibility structure consists of the sum of the rituals and practices that serve to confirm and legitimate the inhabitant's beliefs about a particular social world.

An example may be in order. Within the soldier's social milieu, there exists a plausibility structure that provides justification of and explanation for every detail of military life and belief. There are, most importantly, "significant others" (especially authority figures like commanding officers, chaplains, and physicians) who confirm by their attitudes and assumptions the reality of the military meanings. There are formal ceremonies solemnly enacted as reaffirmations of those meanings, e.g., the awards ceremonies in which medals, citations, and promotions are publicly presented. Informal rituals also form a part of the military's plausibility structure. The "GI party,' in which a soldier whose personal habits of cleanliness do not meet military specifications is abducted by his platoon members and scrubbed from head to toe with wire brushes, is one such ritual. And, of course, there are mechanisms of punishment which unambiguously function to eradicate doubts—and, sometimes, the doubter. These range in severity from reprimands (Article 15s) to reductions in rank and pay, court-martials, stockade sentences, and even, during wartime, death by firing squad. Taken together, these constitute the plausibility structure in and through which the objectivations of the military are maintained.

Conversely, it is through the disintegration of plausibility structures that meanings become eviscerated, or, in the jargon, de-objectivated. In such a situation the assertions that once had the status of objective reality (taken-for-granted knowledge) become more and more problematic. Uncertainty, doubts, questions, and confusions arise in the consciousness of the inhabitants of a tottering plausibility structure. Witness, for example, an anecdote related by a soldier in Vietnam: "We stood there at attention in the morning sun and dust, listening to this fucking asshole do a little memorial service about how 'These people did not die in vain.' If looks could have killed, that man would have been dead. In fact, that man would have been dead if we had been left alone with him. We'd have jumped on him like crows on a corpse" (N, p. 240). Obviously, the plausibility structure designed to maintain the objectivation in question (the nobility of sacrifice in war) has broken down and an aspect of the meaning system has been de-objectivated.

It should now be clearer how the sociology of knowledge perspective may be applied to the situation that interests us here. We contend that the experience of soldiers in Vietnam, as recounted in the literature, can best be grasped as a massive exercise in the de-objectivation of the meanings associated with warfare brought to Vietnam from the United States. More specifically, we wish to show that the conditions under which the fighting in Vietnam took place caused a massive and systematic disconfirmation of those meanings, what we shall refer to throughout as "the retreat from meaning." Finally, we will explore the outcome of this retreat by investigating the meaning system which the soldiers fashioned out of the materials of social experience available to them in Vietnam. This "replacement" meaning system, rooted in instinct, gave form to the Americans' experience in the war zone. In short, we will attempt to reconstruct the cognitive path that the initiate of the preceding chapter traversed, from complex ideas of honor, duty, heroism, and morality to the simple and urgent notion of personal survival.

The Formless War

> My initial exposure the first couple of months I was over there were sort of unrealities. . . . What I thought it was going to be and what it turned out to be were so totally different. There was no romance in it. Absolutely none. That was stripped bare immediately. The whole experience is so different from anything you think it is going to be. You watch John Wayne movies—and it just wasn't the case.
>
> —*Everything We Had*, p. 90

> It seemed odd. We weren't the old soldiers of World War II. No valor to squander for things like country or honor or military objectives. . . . Horace's old do-or-die aphorism—*D[u]lce et decorum est pro patria mori*—was just an epitaph for the insane.
>
> —*If I Die in a Combat Zone*, p. 174

> What the hell am I doing out here, anyway? Where's the goddamn ARVNs? Who needs this shit, huh? I ain't any hero. Goddamn John Wayne, anyway.
>
> —*Fields of Fire*, p. 169

Perhaps nothing contributed more to the retreat from meaning in Vietnam than the military strategy (or lack thereof) employed by the United States Armed Forces. Although the average American assigned to combat duty in Southeast Asia was hardly a subtle military tactician, it scarcely required the genius of a Clausewitz to appreciate the futility in which the GI engaged. That his efforts had little value and thus could not possibly alter the course or duration of the war became obvious immediately. This fact, echoed in every text in the Vietnam canon, was the most powerful factor contributing to the de-objectivation of WWII notions of warfare—the retreat from meaning.

At the very outset, it was clear to the soldiers that the war in Indochina was not being conducted in terms of the glory-myths on which they had been raised. Instead of decisive battles, crucial targets, or even a recognizable army to destroy, "the war in Vietnam drifted in and out of human lives, taking them or sparing them like a headless, beserk taxi hack, without evident cause, a war fought for uncertain reasons" (*IID*, p. 139). Moreover, the Vietnam War never made sense in terms that might be called its own because those terms were "vague, false, or nonexistent. You work that over in your mind for a while and you start to feel pretty rotten" (*FFZ*, p. 86).

The fundamentally different kind of war which Americans fought in Vietnam is best articulated in two succinct formulations culled from the narratives:

The American forces in Vietnam and their allies hunt an enemy in a war that has no front lines. Conventional military objectives, confronting and overpowering the enemy army, capturing strategic areas, are barely recognizable. Thus the development of new standards of success: the number of villages that have succumbed to "search and destroy" missions and an index that is perhaps unprecedented in the history of warfare, the body count (*CWA*, p. 10).

It is not a war fought for territory, nor for pieces of land that will be won and held. It is not a war fought to win the hearts of the Vietnamese nationals, not in the wake of contempt drawn on our faces and on theirs, not in the wake of a burning village, a trampled rice paddy, a battered detainee. If land is not won and if hearts and minds are at best left indifferent, the only obvious criterion of military success is the body count (*IID*, p. 131).

There are a number of salient features in these two descriptions. The most significant is that the war was perceived as formless, without order and purpose, obeying none of the dictates of war logic that a generation of Americans had come to accept as proper and fitting. Rather, the Vietnam War was conducted as a series of "contacts" with the enemy—brief, ferocious, unpredictable—which, the soldiers agree, were pointless. "The insanity was not so much in the events, but that they were undirected, without aim or reason. They happened merely because they happened. The only meaning was in the thing itself" (*FF*, p. 200). This perception dramatizes how the Vietnam War defied efforts to subsume it under both the practical and idealistic categories of World War II. Unable to rationalize the brute fact of men killing each other more or less randomly and continuously, the certainties the soldiers brought to the war zone deteriorated.

They did not know even the simple things: a sense of victory, or satisfaction, or necessary sacrifice. They did not know the feeling of taking a place and keeping it, securing a village and then raising the flag and calling it a victory. No sense of order or momentum. No front, no rear, no trenches laid out in neat parallels. No Patton rushing for the Rhine, no beachheads to storm and win and hold for the duration. They did not have targets. They did not have a cause. They did not know if it was a war of ideology or economics or hegemony or spite (*GAC*, p. 272).

This confusion provoked the GI's retreat from meaning. The participants viewed the war as shapeless, disjointed, fragmented—a reality wholly other than any they had known or were prepared to meet. It seemed to many as though they had been ripped out of one world in which the familiar order of cause-effect, means-end, premises-conclusions operated and had been transported to another planet for their thirteen-month tour of duty. On that alien planet no such comforting regularities were discernible. As one soldier commented, "It was no orderly campaign, as in Europe, but a war waged in a wilderness without rules or laws. . . . Chance. Pure chance. The one true god of modern war is blind chance" (*RW*, pp. 217, 266).

The GIs' perceptions of the Vietnam War as a separate universe in which the forms of everyday reality are absent are neatly captured in their own linguistic typifications. For the combat troops in Vietnam, reality was classifiable into two distinct domains: "The World" and "The Nam." This latter is viewed as a reality whose contours are neither stable nor determinate. It is a world marked by "an absence of aim and purpose, so that the footsoldier is left without the moral imperatives to fight hard and well and winningly" (*GAC*, p. 198). In addition, events in this reality occur without organic connection one to another, each sealed into itself and inexplicable in terms of the usual interrogatories that suffice in "the world": whither? whence? and why?

Even the most fundamental distinction in the soldierly cosmos—victory or defeat—seemed to have no correspondence to the configuration of events he faced:

> "Do you think we're winning?"
> Gilliland thought about it for a moment. He lit a cigarette and took a drag and thought about it some more. He was somewhat shocked, not by the question, but by the fact that he'd never considered it in his entire second tour. They had never talked about it in the bush. It had nothing to do with being in the bush and fighting gooks. They had talked about good contacts and bad contacts and Getting Some and Bummers. But not about winning (*FF*, p. 230).

The narrators point out the formlessness of their war in a variety of ways, each emphasizing the retreat from meaning. The most frequently adopted strategy for dramatizing the formlessness of their war is through comparison with the "Paradigm War"—WWII. Most disorienting (and de-objectivating) is their apprehension that the traditional goals of war are absent, as are the standards by which to determine effectiveness. The underlying assumption, based on the WWII paradigm, is that war is inescapably eschatological, deriving its meaning from its outcome. In World War II this assumption took the form of an immediately recognizable strategy which was relatively simple to implement: push the enemy back to his point of origin, capture that point of origin, declare yourself triumphant. In its fundamentals, World War II (at least in the European Theatre of operations) was reducible to the single parade ground command, "March!" If one executed that command in the correct direction with appropriate determination, then progress could be gauged in statute miles. War, in this conception, is a relatively manageable affair of front lines, rear areas, hostile armies, and demarcated campaigns. It is war with plot, plan, and pattern. Contrast that rather tidy arrangement with the one presented in the following exchange:

"They say there ain't any front in Vietnam. That right?"
    Gilliland shook his head yes, then no. He smiled hopelessly. "Shit, man. I don't know. I know we used to like to get back to the rear. There was a rear. But we were never on any front, or anything. We just roamed around the bush, or went somewhere on an operation for a while and then left. We just moved in circles, mostly."
    "Sounds crazy."
    "Well, it was. It was crazy as hell." (*FF*, p. 230).

Such dialogue indicates a world in which prior assumptions have been invalidated, a world given, in Schutz's phrase, "further notice."

Soldiers are not traditionally fluent in the language of phenomenological social scientists. Yet soldiers, like all humans, strive to make sense of their experience in accord with the felt needs of their situation. The most basic of those needs is a body of taken-for-granted knowledge that is confirmed by ongoing social activity. As Berger says, "Man is an empirical animal to the extent that his own direct experience is the most convincing evidence of the reality of anything."[11] In Vietnam, the GIs' experiences served to disconfirm their previously held assumptions. Their belief, based on WWII lore, that "we were going to win the war in a few months and then march home to ticker-tape parades" (*RW*, p. 180), gave way to the recognition that "this is Vietnam, this isn't World War Two where we can pull you out to a parade after a month of fighting" (*FF*, p. 68). As one soldier laments this retreat from meaning:

Writing about this kind of warfare is not a simple task. Repeatedly, I have found myself wishing that I had been the veteran of a conventional war, with dramatic campaigns and historic battles for subject matter instead of a monotonous succession of ambushes and fire-fights. But there were no Normandies or Gettysburgs for us, no epic clashes that decided the fates of armies or nations. The war was mostly a matter of enduring weeks of expectant waiting and, at random intervals, of conducting vicious manhunts through jungles and swamps where snipers harassed us constantly and booby traps cut us down one by one (*RW*, p. xiv).

This elegy for the war-with-form and exasperation with the formless war is echoed throughout the narratives.

The formless war did have its own distinctive contours, although those contours became visible only in retrospect. The Vietnam War was perceived as formless because of the discrepancy between the loose form it took and the form the soldiers had been trained to identify and label as such. This unfamiliar form involved two sorts of combat engagements, the "fire-fight" and the "search and destroy" mission, neither of which conformed to WWII battle scenarios.

The fire-fight was simply a furious exchange of shots between belligerents. Referred to as "the Mad Minute" (*D*, p. 62), it had no strategic aim beyond inflicting casualties. A fire-fight usually occurred as a sudden, unplanned event, the result of ambush or accident. The GIs report that fire-fights erupted and subsided randomly and changed nothing except the number of corpses that had to be bagged, tagged, and shipped back to "the World." The essentially sporadic and purposeless nature of the fire-fight gave impetus to the retreat from meaning. Those who expected glorious battles were quickly disappointed: "Our first experience of combat had not turned out the way we imagined it would. Used to the orderly sham battles of field exercises, the real thing proved to be more chaotic and much less heroic than we anticipated. . . . It was a haphazard, episodic sort of combat. Most of the time nothing happened, but when something did it happened instantaneously and without warning" (*RW*, pp. 120, 89).

It did not take long for the soldiers to realize that the fire-fights weren't at all analogous to the heroic charges and decisive confrontations of their fathers' war. In fact, it quickly became evident that the fire-fight didn't result in any discernible difference beyond the casualties produced. One soldier described it thusly: "In a fire-fight you got twenty guys over there shooting at you and you got twenty or thirty guys over here shooting back at them. We'll call in artillery fire. They're call-

ing in mortar fire. Somebody decides, 'Okay, I've had enough.'
Then that's over. But there was no ground taken. Nobody won
anything or moved their lines" (*N*, p. 110). This kind of aimless fighting was so foreign to the WWII image of set-piece
battles that it prompted one infantryman to remark, "Combat, I hadn't seen no combat. All I seen was guys getting killed"
(*Fr. F*, p. 380).

If the fire-fight de-objectivated WWII notions of glory, the
other sort of contact with the enemy—the search and destroy
mission—dealt a *coup de grâce* to WWII ideas of morality. As
we have seen, Americans were initiated to believe that they
embodied absolute good in the role of savior. Although the fire-
fight threatened established meanings because it was inconclusive—"nothing changed beyond the tragedy of the immediate event" (*FF*, p. 199)—the search and destroy tactic had just
the opposite defect: it was irrevocable. The spirit of search and
destroy was massive destruction. Ostensibly, the goal of these
missions was to flush out the enemy by denying him refuge.
In practice, however, it was "more a gestalt than a tactic . . .
we were there to bring them the choice, bringing it to them
like Sherman bringing the Jubilee through Georgia, clean
through it, wall to wall with pacified indigenous and scorched
earth" (*D*, pp. 61, 43).

Search and destroy was the product of the same military
mentality associated with the destruction of Dresden and Hiroshima. However, in Vietnam it was wretched excessiveness
on a regular basis. (By 1969, North Vietnam was being hit each
month with an explosive force equal to two atomic bombs.) One
soldier describes it, "It was a search-and-destroy mission, which
meant we searched all the hootches we found and burned them
down. Whether a single farmer's hootch or a whole village—
all were burnt" (*TKZ*, p. 31). Another recalls, "My last tour we'd
go through and that was it, we'd rip out the hedges and burn
the hootches and blow all the wells and kill every chicken, pig
and cow in the whole fucking ville" (*D*, p. 29).

For American soldiers trained to understand their role in
Vietnam as saviors, the daily experience of search and destroy
gave the lie to that belief: "And the village itself was burned.
What was left after the burning was dynamited, it was plowed

into the ground and the ground was salted. I went to Ben Suc about a week after this happened in a convoy, and there was nothing there except bare, burned earth. That was what was left of Ben Suc and it had been done by Americans. I never saw the Vietcong do anything like that" (*CWA*, p. 86). Indeed, it quickly became obvious that carrying out search and destroy missions was tantamount to recruiting for the Vietcong: "Now, when they [First Platoon] get inside that ville, they're gonna burn it down. . . . I figure [First Platoon] done *made* a lot more VC than they ever end up killing" (*FF*, p. 171). In a war in which the "good guys" behave in ways characteristic of the "bad guys," no notion of American morality could survive.

The mechanics of search and destroy were not only brutal, they were also arbitrary. A village that one day was considered "friendly," i.e., inhabited by Vietnamese loyal to the Government of South Vietnam (GVN), could be reclassified a "contested area" the next day and marked for destruction. Overnight, in some instances, large areas of the countryside were designated "free-fire zones" in which any living thing was presumed hostile and could be blown up, often without the inhabitants ever being informed of their new status as targets: "And I asked my Captain what was going to happen to the people we just helped for a month and a half, build their village and treat them and train them. He says, 'Well, as far as we are concerned, they are VC's.' The next day you could see the village was completely wiped out" (*CWA*, p. 118). In the never-never-land terminology that came to characterize U. S. involvement in Southeast Asia, a hamlet that had suffered such treatment would be officially reclassified as "pacified."* Thus, the only planned activity conducted on the ground by the U. S. military in the formless war was, in the words of one veteran, "not warfare, it was murder" (*RW*, p. 272).

---

*With his usual prescience, George Orwell anticipated the mutilation of language in the service of inhumanity. In *A Collection of Essays*, published in 1954, the same year that the French were slaughtered at Dien Bien Phu, Orwell wrote, "Defenseless villages are bombarded from the air, the inhabitants driven out into the countryside, the cattle machinegunned, the huts set on fire with incendiary bullets: This is called *pacification*"

The formless war forced a recognition that WWII beliefs were hopelessly inadequate for rendering experience intelligible. The randomness and aimlessness of the fire-fight and the sheer perversity of the search and destroy strategy caused a whole-sale retreat from meaning. The soldiers, of course, never talk about de-objectivation or the collapse of plausibility struc-tures. Their own linguistic categories, however, reveal the transformation of world view these social science neologisms are designed to convey. They speak, that is, of a world now perceived as *senseless* and *absurd*, of a war in which "there was no real military objective" (*EWH*, p. 137).

The soldiers' reliance on the term *senseless* points specifi-cally to their thwarted expectations. "Sense," what we have called "meaning," designates a satisfactory fit between the GIs' anticipations and the realities they faced in their everyday endeavors. That fit was virtually nonexistent in Vietnam. In the troops' own words, "it was beginning to make less and less sense. . . . You just wander around trying to kill them until they kill you. . . . Where the hell is the sense in that? It's in-sane" (*FF*, p. 117). "He was a young guy. He had received word in the mail the week before from his wife that his first baby had been born. Senseless, needless. All wars are filled with that. But there was more of it in Vietnam. Or maybe because the whole thing was so senseless, every time something like that happened it was just another insult" (*N*, p. 240). "There was nobody in this village, only an old couple. . . . It made no sense, absolutely no sense to me, why this village was there, why this old couple was there, why they were killing. . . . I just couldn't put it together" (*EWH*, p. 117). "There was really no sense in it, you know" (*CWA*, p. 313).

Thus, U. S. military strategy, which one commentator de-scribed as "us looking for him looking for us looking for him, war on a Cracker Jack Box, repeated to diminishing returns" (*D*, p. 61), objectivated the view that "the whole world gets ab-surd after a while" (*N*, p. 94). Like *senseless*, the word *absur-dity* figures prominently in the soldiers' lexicon. "It's absurd. Patent absurdity. The troops are going home and the war has not been won, even with a quarter of the United States Army fighting it. We slay one of them, hit a mine, kill another, hit another mine" (*IID*, p. 129). Their own immediate experience in the formless war convinced the GIs of its absurdity: "I made corporal when we took this hill called Razorback three times. We would go up there, spend a week and leave. Each time we lost men. There ain't nothing on that stupid-ass hill. It's out in the middle of bullshit. Walk up it getting killed and walk down the other side again. We did that three times" (*N*, p. 233).

In a war in which "nothing's what it's s'posed to be" (*FF*, p. 101), and men are required to behave on the basis of "an absurd combination of certainty and uncertainty" (*IID*, p. 127), even death "can no longer be accorded a certain sum of dignity" (*FF*, p. 199). Dying in the formless war was stripped of the meanings which traditionally adhere to sacrifice during times of national emergency. Because the war was perceived as "senseless" and "absurd," serving no discernible purpose and benefitting no human community, death in it was a purely physical event, bereft of larger import. Most frequently, death was viewed as simply bad luck. As one soldier recalls, "They seemed to have died for nothing; if not for nothing, then for nothing tangible. Those men might as well have died in automobile accidents" (*RW*, p. 191). This view was reflected in the GIs' vocabulary: "In that war a soldier's slang for death was 'wasted.' So-and-so was wasted. It was a good word" (*RW*, pp. 209–10). "No one used the words 'die' and 'death.' A man was hit, not wounded. If he was killed, they said wasted or blown-away. He bought it or bought the farm. He was greased or lit-up. Death was the Max" (*WL*, p. 64).

In the formless war—where combat is either random and inconclusive or capricious and morally noxious—a tradition of dying died. Rather than grandeur and nobility, death in rice paddies and jungles "don't mean nothing, really. It's just a game" (*FF*, p. 101). One combatant, describing his own retreat from meaning, said, "The sight of mutilation did more than cause me physical revulsion; it burst the religious myths of my Catholic childhood. I could not look at those men and still believe their souls had 'passed on' to another existence, or that they had had souls in the first place" (*RW*, p. 121). Such a drastic de-objectivation was possible because the soldiers' daily experiences convinced them that "the number of dead meant

nothing, changed nothing" (*D*, p. 96) and that "beyond adding
a few more corpses to the weekly body count, none of these
encounters achieved anything" (*RW*, p. xv). In a situation in
which "a lot of people are getting killed and you don't know
why" (*CWA*, p. 178), meanings invested in death by the military milieu topple. Once those meanings collapse, the inhabitants of that milieu "feel more like victims than soldiers" (*RW*,
p. 272).

One especially grotesque aspect of the formless war that deprived the ideas of "Glory and War and Honored Dead" (*D*,
p. 105) of plausibility was the constant risk of meeting death
at the hands of one's comrades, what the military called "non-
hostile causes."[12] Because the Vietnam War relied heavily upon
the most sophisticated technological weaponry, much of it
previously untested under the pressures of actual combat, there
were inevitable human and mechanical failures.[13] In addition
to the ordnance itself, the novel ways in which it was deployed in Vietnam carried unknown dangers. The "air-mobile"
concept, for instance, which replaced the WWII jeep with the
helicopter for transporting personnel into combat, was peril-
ous in a way unimagined by the desk-bound tacticians back at
the Pentagon. Indeed, the use of massive airpower of all kinds,
from the helicopter assault to the supportive airstrike to car-
pet-bombing, greatly increased the odds of suffering death
"accidentally."[14]

Such an accidental demise, dealt blindly, often by unseen
forces miles above or away from the soldier whose life was en-
dangered, rendered death more probably ironic than heroic. In
fact, for the common foot soldier the high-technology facet of
the formless war posed unprecedented problems of explanation. As one soldier outlines the quandary in moral terms,

According to those "rules of engagement," it was morally right to shoot
an unarmed Vietnamese who was running, but wrong to shoot one
who was standing or walking; it was wrong to shoot an enemy prisoner at close range, but right for a sniper at long range to kill an
enemy soldier who was no more able than a prisoner to defend himself; it was wrong for infantrymen to destroy a village with white-
phosphorous grenades, but right for a fighter pilot to drop napalm on

it. Ethics seemed to be a matter of distance and technology. You could never go wrong if you killed people at long range with sophisticated weapons (*RW*, p. 218).

Ethical considerations aside, the immediate consequence of such blind destructive capacity was to make the environment appear completely lethal. It often seemed as if all the forces of man and nature had conspired to take the life of the GI in the bush. Upon hearing the sound of an unmistakably American artillery shell land nearby, a soldier expressed a perception common in the war zone: "That was our own gun. They're all trying to kill us. They want us dead. Everybody wants us dead" (*FF*, p. 146). Others furnish testimony of just such a reality: "Marines ambushing Marines, artillery and airstrikes called in on our own positions, all in the course of routine Search-and-Destroy operations. And you knew that sooner or later it would happen to you, too" (*D*, p. 102); "misdirected artillery, tanks moving in to destroy a bunker and it would run over our own wounded without regard for whether or not they were laying there, and it really got to the point of the ridiculous all the time. Things like that were always happening" (*CWA*, p. 211); "Those stupid sons of bitches! They're supposed to be shooting out there, but they're shooting at us. If we'd have given ourselves as a target, they couldn't have done any better" (*Fr. F*, p. 362). As one bitter warrior put it, "Whenever the VC duck we shoot each other" (*M*, p. 167). In an ultimate absurdity, U. S. Forces would attempt to retaliate against their own countrymen who had inflicted such "non-hostile" damage: "Two Marine gunships came down on us and began strafing us, sending burning tracers up along the canal, and we ran for cover, more surprised than scared. 'Way to go, motherfucker, way to pin-point the fuckin' enemy,' one of the grunts said, and he set up his M–60 machine gun in case they came back. 'I don't guess we gotta take *that* shit,' he said" (*D*, p. 75).

Under such conditions, death loses its culturally derived meaning as an ultimate event and particularly its military connotation as "sacrifice in the line of duty." Rather, death is viewed simply as the cessation of biological viability, the result of mishap. "Something always went wrong somewhere, somehow. It was always something vague, unexplainable, tasting of bad fate, and the results were always brought down to their basic element—the dead Marine" (*D*, p. 102). Only under the sway of such a world view, where high ideals have been drained of substantive content, could the soldiers themselves self-mockingly author a hymn to be delivered to a dead Marine's mother that went, "Tough shit, tough shit, your kid got greased, but what the fuck, he was just a dumb grunt" (*D*, p. 103).

By focusing attention on the novel conditions which obtained in Vietnam, we have tried to demonstrate how the war's formlessness fueled the de-objectivation of WWII meanings. The confounding of cognitive structures for explaining war forced the GIs into a retreat from meaning. We might go further in this analysis and insist that the fundamental task of any society, even (or perhaps especially) during war, is to furnish order, to provide forms for experience. Such order provides meaning without which members of a society are overwhelmed in their ongoing encounter with the world. Order is integral to every society, and all social institutions are geared to the maintenance of social forms. This fact is especially apparent if we consider the most basic social institution out of which all others flourish: language. Language provides the fundamental assortment of categories under which to subsume experience. Through language, and especially "conversation" as we used that term earlier, objectivation occurs and reality is constructed and construed. This process is true of all the other social institutions which carry the task forward at different levels of abstraction. All cooperate in the cause of *nomos*, i.e., ordering.

Peter Berger goes so far as to assert that the human need for order has its roots in man's biological constitution.[15] Whether or not this is so, it is clear that "order is the primary imperative of social life" and further that "society, in its essence, is the imposition of order on the flux of experience."[16] A recognition of this feature of man's nature may give us some intellectual leverage for grasping adequately the full impact which the formless war had on those who experienced it. For if the imposition of recognizable form is universally necessary for human social life, then the desuetude of form is terrifying. Given the shapelessness of the war experience, its moral, tactical, and technological amorphousness, we would expect meanings constructed in an orderly environment to lose plausibility rapidly. Indeed, this is precisely what we have witnessed as we have followed the soldiers into the vastly altered social surround of the war zone.

One text in the Vietnam canon, *One Very Hot Day* by David Halberstam, stands out especially in this context. Halberstam makes precise and explicit the comparison between the Second World War and the Vietnam War. By doing so, he dramatizes the ineluctably meaning-subverting nature of the war in Indochina. Such a comparison shows the Vietnam War for what the soldiers experienced it as: a crusade against meaning rather than for hearts and minds.

Told through the eyes of Captain Beauchamp, an aging, overweight, and washed-up career officer given to strong drink, *One Very Hot Day* depicts a world and a war that fail to conform to the dictates of logical order, a world in which "you began with distrust, you assumed it about everything, even things you thought you knew" (*VHD*, p. 127). This world is one which stands in marked contrast to World War II and Korea, in which Beauchamp prides himself on having fought. It is no secret that Beauchamp's disgust and revulsion for the Vietnam War reflect Halberstam's own. (Beauchamp was modeled on an officer Halberstam met during his coverage of the Vietnam War. His sentiments are not literally Halberstam's.)

As a correspondent for the *New York Times* Halberstam was among the first in the press corps to submit unfavorable reports on the American initiative in Vietnam from the field. President Kennedy attempted unsuccessfully to have the *Times* recall Halberstam in 1962.[17] Halberstam remained in Indochina to cover the war and also authored *The Best and the Brightest*, a stunning indictment of the people and policies that led to the debacle in Southeast Asia.[18]

One Very Hot Day conveys a sense of how the U. S. employed a hopelessly inadequate military strategy that generated chaos. The flabby but war-wise Beauchamp spends a goodly portion of the novel reminiscing about the Second World

War, offering comparisons that bring into bold relief how traditional military tactics serve, among other aims, as part of the plausibility structure that maintains a soldier's world view. Without those tactics to confirm a soldierly reality, the meanings attached to war disintegrate. He says of the war against Hitler, "We didn't know how simple it was and how good we had it. Sure we walked, but in a straight line. Normandy beaches and then you set off for Paris and Berlin. Just like that. No retracing, no goddamn circles, just straight ahead. All you needed was a compass and good sense. But here you walk in a goddamn circle and then you go home and then you go out the next day and wade through a circle, and then you go home and the next day you go out and you reverse the circle you did the day before, erasing it" (*VHD*, p. 114). The frustration, futility, and bewilderment associated with military maneuvers in Vietnam de-mythologized WWII meanings.

When Beauchamp "had first arrived, he had brought with him a sense of total tension and tautness fashioned out of WWII and Korea" (*VHD*, p. 88), what we might designate the affective components of a plausibility structure legitimating traditional meanings. These emotions, Beauchamp discovers, are ill suited to his third war. Most urgently required in the Vietnam conflict is "an ability to roll with it and feel its pace" (*VHD*, p. 88). That particular pace renders procedures borrowed from other wars self-defeating. Although in WWII it made perfect sense to rush headlong in pursuit of one's clearly designated foe, in Vietnam an altogether different logic applied. Unlike the war "in France where you always knew where you were, how far you had walked, how far you had to go" (*VHD*, p. 114), in Vietnam "one would have to be a raving maniac if he spent his first three operations chasing VC everywhere; by the fourth he would be in a state of physical and mental exhaustion and, of course, Charlie would step out and zap him. It was a lousy goddamn war" (*VHD*, p. 89). This inability to dictate the terms of the fighting, to control the course of the war in any significant way, is a powerful factor spurring the retreat from meaning.

Vietnam, as Beauchamp realizes, is the site of "this new world and this new Army" in which "even the Americans seemed different to him now and he trusted them less. They had changed. Yes was no longer yes, no was no longer exactly no, maybe was more certainly maybe" (*VHD*, p. 127). The nature of reality is more ambiguous as the taken-for-granted objectivations lose plausibility. Language, as an index of cultural reality, reflects this new uncertainty. In this situation, one's knowledge is no longer trustworthy, because appearances may belie the underlying reality. Reality therefore becomes problematic and potentially deceptive. Beauchamp's complaint about the instability of linguistic meanings articulates the very essence of the retreat from meaning. It is a cry of bewilderment in the face of evaporating forms through which to interpret experience.

Beauchamp's cognitive difficulties are clearly not with fighting per se. He holds no brief for pacifism, as did so many civilian critics of the Vietnam War. Rather, his frustration is with "the senselessness of the war—not the killing but the endless walking each day and returning to My Tho with nothing done, nothing seen, nothing accomplished, nothing changed, just hiking each day with death, taking chances for so very little" (*VHD*, p. 126). This brutal recognition that one could "die for nothing" is echoed throughout the Vietnam narratives. As a result of such a drastic de-objectivation of the military meaning of sacrifice, physical survival takes on ultimate meaning.

This obsession with survival as the biological bottom line of meaning in Vietnam is precisely what Beauchamp comes to comprehend and endorse. It is this facet of the "lousy goddamn war" that distinguishes it from the other military campaigns in which he had previously served. The meanings carried over from those campaigns are progressively stripped of plausibility by the daily activities in which he engages. As these meanings become inoperative, meaning comes, by default as it were, to be located in the visceral responses of an organism struggling for self-preservation: "What was coming awake in him was a deep sense of survival . . . it was as if there were a great reservoir of survival instinct in him which was now being tapped" (*VHD*, p. 154). Given Beauchamp's understanding of Vietnam's radical discontinuity with past wars, he is tempted to share his hard-won knowledge that the war's "true" meaning is reducible to the single, mindless imperative of survival. He wishes especially to convince his comrades that the meanings they hold are unsuited to this war: "He sometimes wanted to reach out to them and tell them that they had been badly briefed, that none of it was true, that it was the cautious ones who would live and survive, and make it home to give the briefings, and it is the cautious ones who get ahead" (*VHD*, p. 89). This belief is neither easily proclaimed nor readily accepted by the other soldiers. Their initiation, the "briefing" given them by American culture, has ill equipped them to grasp their situation: "But those who survived would have to learn for themselves, or not learn for themselves" (*VHD*, p. 89).

This learning process actually happens as the "one very hot day" comprising the novel's entire time span reaches its dramatic climax. Beauchamp's young second-in-command, Lieutenant Anderson, has throughout the book stuck rigidly by the world view of his alma mater, West Point. Full of the Point's creed of glory-duty-honor, Lt. Anderson has been briefed in a way that makes him unable to appreciate the nature, and hence survive the duration, of this war. In spite of Beauchamp's efforts, Anderson is killed in an ambush on a routine patrol in the jungle. Anderson's death on that particular very hot day reeks of nothing more than tragic waste. It results in no discernible difference in attaining a nonexistent objective. With the death of his gung-ho protégé, Beauchamp jettisons the ballast of WWII meanings he brought to Vietnam, and the formless war claims two more casualties: Lt. Anderson's body and Capt. Beauchamp's world view.

Halberstam's war novel concisely points up what in the Vietnam War provoked the retreat from meaning. Besides dramatizing the war's formlessness, Halberstam addresses prominent features of the war which we will analyze in the remainder of this chapter. If we are fully to comprehend the retreat from meaning, we must examine the de-objectivation of WWII meanings and the disintegration of the plausibility structures that maintained them. This process entails examining not only how the war was fought but also against whom and with what results. We, like the struggling Beauchamp, must attempt to understand the nature of the enemy, the banality of death, and the utter urgency of nothing but pure survival.

The Invisible Enemy

In this way Demergian came to appreciate the eerie nature of his generation's war. On many, *most* of the veterans in Vietnam, one will discern an uneasy flitting of the eyes or an irresolute twitch at the corners of the mouth, it testifies how they've been a year in the field boxing shadows, taking up arms against a sea of unseen essences, locked in combat with an insubstantial Kafkan vapor . . .

—*M*, p. 150

The VC would be the farmer you waved to from your jeep in the day who would be the guy with the gun out looking for you at night. . . . The big problem was you couldn't find the enemy. It was very frustrating because how do you fight back against a booby-trap?

—*Everything We Had*, p. 49

In the patriotic fervor of the Kennedy years we had asked, "What can we do for our country?" and our country answered, "Kill VC."

—*A Rumor of War*, p. 218

The particular rigors of counterinsurgency warfare have been alluded to repeatedly throughout the preceding pages. It is now necessary to examine in greater detail the unique responses this type of fighting demands of combatants prepared, virtually from childhood, to engage in a conventional war. American soldiers had been taught that they were going to war to kill Communists, the very incarnation of evil. Unfortunately for those soldiers, the characteristic beliefs by which Communists can be clearly identified—especially in Vietnam—are not open to inspection and therefore do not distinguish them

from the general populace. Without any signs of political lean-
ings to mark off the Communist Oriental from his democracy-
loving counterpart, the American GI faced the difficult task of
adjudicating life-and-death differences (very likely *his own* life
or death) on the basis of identical appearances. At least one of
the consequences of this indeterminacy were atrocities committed by Americans on a scale unimaginable before Vietnam.

The enemy's effectiveness had little to do with any purely
material military advantage. Undeniably, the training, equipment, support, and manpower of the U. S. forces in Indochina
were substantially superior to the NVAs' or the VCs'. What
the Vietnamese nationalists, in their latest incarnation as the
Vietcong, did possess was extensive experience in fighting a
type of war where stealth, evasion, elusiveness, and the element of surprise counted more heavily than did conventional
indices of military might.

The VC and NVA relied upon the tactics of guerilla warfare
which enabled them to seize the initiative in virtually every
situation wherein they encountered U. S. forces. Specifically,
the VC were highly mobile, well disciplined, and, most importantly, *undetectable until they attacked*. This last characteristic, which we shall denominate "the invisible enemy," influ-
enced the soldiers in a way that contributed enormously to their
retreat from meaning. Blending in among the civilian population, often holding positions of authority in the government
and military of the regime they were pledged to destroy, the
insurgents could dictate the time, place, and numbers of a
contact with virtual impunity. Using surprise as their principal weapon, the VC repeatedly managed to strike, inflict severe damage, and fade back into anonymity before an appropriate military response could be mounted.

In addition to their uncanny ability to launch an offensive
and then seemingly evaporate, the VC relied heavily upon
ordnance that could be cheaply produced, easily distributed,
and effectively deployed to extract an enormous psychological
and physical toll. We are referring to the booby trap, perhaps
the most psychologically devastating anti-personnel weapon in
the modern military arsenal. Unlike the conventional WWII
battles in which opposing armies squared off to fight each other
to unqualified victory or defeat, many of the casualties in

Vietnam were inflicted by invisible or innocent-looking devices planted days or weeks before by an enemy who had long
since fled. These devices, triggered by inadvertent contact, were
particularly terrifying because little can be done to defend
against the hideous wounds they are capable of inflicting. The
soldiers lived in unending fear that each step or movement
might trigger such a trap and release its capacity to deliver
grotesque injury.* One soldier perceptively analyzed the de-
moralizing and meaning-subverting aspect of this kind of
warfare.

We *were* making history: the first American soldiers to fight an enemy whose principal weapons were the mine and the booby trap. That
kind of warfare has its own peculiar terrors. It turns an infantryman's world upside down. The foot soldier has a special feeling for
the ground. He walks on it, fights on it, sleeps and eats on it; the
ground shelters him under fire; he digs his home in it. But mines
and booby traps transform that friendly, familiar earth into a thing
of menace, a thing to be feared as much as machine guns or mortar
shells. The infantryman knows that any moment the ground he is
walking on can erupt and kill him; kill him if he is lucky. If he's un-
lucky, he will be turned into a blind, deaf, emasculated, legless
shell. . . . We could not fight back against the Viet Cong mines or
take cover from them or anticipate when they would go off (*RW*,
pp. 272–73).

Such testimony accentuates another component underlying
the retreat from meaning. Just as the formless war thwarted

---

*The bouncing-betty, for instance, rigged to spring out of the ground and det-
onate at waist level, inflicted grotesque wounds. As one soldier described them,
"They were trip mines. All you had to do was bury them and pull the pin. You
could rig them up sixteen different ways. Step on them and they usually go
off waist-high. It's a 60-millimeter mortar round, called a daisy cutter, with a
super fast fuse, designed to go off in a flat disc explosion. Bouncing Betty . . .
it's supposed to cut you in half, groin level. It's a psychological thing . . . and
we had to go out and find them one at a time. Meaning, BOOM" (*EWH*, p. 30).
An even more primitive, and ghastly, anti-personnel device was the "punji pit,"
a ditch filled with sharpened bamboo spikes the tips of which were dipped in
excrement (to ensure blood poisoning). These pits remained concealed by fo-
liage until an unsuspecting soldier had fallen into one. A variation of the punji
pit used punji stakes rigged to bent branches of trees. A GI, pushing aside
some undergrowth, would release the punji stick directly into his face.

the fundamental human need for order, the threat posed by
the invisible enemy undermined an equally basic imperative
of human existence: triviality. Peter Berger insists that "triviality is one of the fundamental requirements of social life" because "social life would be psychologically intolerable if each
of its moments required from us full attention."[19] Triviality is,
in fact, an intended consequence of the order that social institutions impose. It serves to preempt the number of choices
humans must confront. Because order enables men to take for
granted the constructed regularities of their social world, they
are able to conduct a large portion of their lives in a state of
dim awareness. In the same manner that order protects the
individual from being engulfed by a terrifying chaos, triviality
shields the individual from the agony of constant alertness. "If
social life in its entirety were charged with profound meaning,
we would all go out of our minds."[20] Societies thus protect their
members from the nightmare of frequent "significant events"
by establishing large areas of everyday life in which routine,
habit, ritual—varying forms of repetition—shield the individual from the necessity of attending to all aspects of ongoing
activity. Again, whether or not such a "trivializing" process is
biologically necessary, it is clear that man's attention span is
limited and that he can only tolerate a limited amount of ex-
citement.

What emerges from an examination of the soldiers' narrative accounts is a world in which this fundamental human need
is frustrated. The presence of the invisible enemy forced soldiers to maintain an excruciating level of awareness. In Vietnam, each moment might require responses upon which life
or death hung in the balance. "That was one of the things that
made the war such a nerve-jangling experience: the constant
and total uncertainty. Whether we were going out on a squad
patrol or into a battalion-sized attack, we never knew what
we were going to run into. We were always tense with the
feeling that anything could happen at any moment" (RW,
p. 272). Even such a simple activity as walking—in "the World"
regarded as perfectly "trivial"—could require full alertness of
"your every movement of which way to shift your weight, of
where to sit down" (IID, p. 127). As a platoon leader said of
his men, "In the sodden world they inhabited, the mere act of

walking, an act almost as unconscious as breathing, could bring
death" (*RW*, p. 223).

Such taxing awareness, even if cultivated, didn't guarantee
safety because the enemy picked the times and places to strike.
"They never fought back until they were ready, but we had to
pursue and attempt to engage every slightest vision" (*FF*,
p. 157); "You didn't fight them, you had to wait for them to
want to fight you. Then you had to just protect your butt. They
could get you, but you couldn't move on them conventionally"
(*N*, p. 108); "There was no enemy to fire at, there was nothing
to retaliate against. . . . Phantoms, I thought, we're fighting
phantoms" (*RW*, p. 55); "I could deal with a man. That meant
my talent against his for survival, but how do you deal with
him when he ain't even there?" (*N*, p. 111). The hit-and-run
tactics of "the invisible enemy" made the total concentration
demanded of combat troops an experience of exquisite torture.
In an environment in which paranoid psychosis is a "sane" response—"They were nowhere. They were everywhere" (*FF*,
p. 117)—morale is an instant casualty; "There are so many ways
the VC can do it. So many configurations, so many types of
camouflage to hide them. I'm ready to go home" (*IID*, p. 127).

This already intolerable strain on one's capacity to formulate reasonable judgments was accelerated by the VCs' remarkable success at infiltration. This tactic, essential for successful insurgency, made the Vietnam War cognitively
insufferable to the Americans. The Vietcong, identical in appearance and language to the "friendly" Vietnamese for whom
the Americans were presumably fighting and dying, managed
to become firmly ensconced among the indigenous population
in the South. Like the South Vietnamese loyal to the Saigon
government, the VC sought to earn a livelihood with the area's
largest equal opportunity employer: the United States military. Often this effort included joining the Army of the Republic of Vietnam. For obvious reasons, the ARVN's pay and benefits—subsidized by the United States Military Command-
Vietnam (MACV)—far exceeded those of civilian peasants. One
soldier, upon his arrival in the war zone, ruefully recalls his
difficulty in coping with his first taste of the invisible enemy:
"That a battalion full of VC in ARVN uniforms could be defending an American air base against the VC was still beyond

our understanding" (*RW*, p. 52). Another observes that "the VC
got work inside the camps as shoeshine boys and laundresses
and honey-dippers, they'd starch your fatigues and burn your
shit and then go home and mortar your area" (*D*, p. 14).

The Saigon government, under MACV urging, attempted to
distinguish the loyal Vietnamese from the insurgents by is-
suing I. D. cards. The owner of an identification card (*can cuoc*,
in Vietnamese) was registered with the Saigon government and
was therefore permitted to travel without suffering detain-
ment or interrogation. The failure of a peasant to produce his
I. D. was sufficient grounds for arrest as a "VC suspect." Although this scheme sounded reasonable, in practice it simply
served to exacerbate confusion and render the enemy *more* invisible. A primarily pre-literate farming population, unused to
handling documents of any sort, was not the ideal choice upon
which to impose the forms of modern bureaucracy. *Can cuoc*'s
were frequently lost, left at home because of the enormous difficulty of securing a replacement, or simply traded for a more
immediately utilitarian item like a kilo of rice. Also, the VC
printed their own counterfeit identification cards which en-
sured their safe passage, frequently with ARVN escort, through
the war-torn countryside. The effort to foil the invisible enemy's assimilation into society is dramatized in the following
interchange:

"Oh. *Him*? He lost his *can cuoc*." Phony noted that the phrase did not
register with Hodges. "His I. D. card." He put his arm around the old
man's shoulders. "It's a lifer game. Find a dude without his *can cuoc*
and he's s'posed to be VC or something, 'cause he ain't registered with
the gov'mint."

Snake had joined the group. He addressed Hodges. "So every time
we find a dude without one, we're s'posed to run him in. But it's like
everything out here, Lieutenant. Nothing's what it's s'posed to be. All
the VC have *can cuocs*. Half the villagers don't, cause when you lose
it, you have to pay a goddamn fortune to get a new one. So *can cuocs*
don't mean nothing, really. It's just a game" (*FF*, p. 101).

In the words of one soldier, "It's very common for the Vietnamese to not have their ID cards. We learned that after
awhile. At first we thought it was the most heinous crime in
the world, not carrying your ID card" (*CWA*, p. 158).

The invisible enemy posed a constant threat to life and limb (and meaning). The contours of reality become especially vague when even the fundamental distinction between civilian and soldier cannot be confidently made. As one soldier put it, "We had crossed that line between a world of relative stability and one that was wholly unstable; the world where anything could happen at any moment" (*RW*, p. 122).

In the conventional model of war upon which the American GI was raised, vast numbers of the population could be regarded as neutral (civilian non-combatants) presenting the GI with no immediate physical danger. In Vietnam, no such category existed. The enemy in Vietnam wore no uniforms, nor did it abide by the rules of engagement of conventional wars in which there are designated nonbelligerents. In short, "there was no reliable criterion by which to distinguish a pretty Vietnamese girl from a deadly enemy; often they were one and the same person" (*IID*, p. 119). In this deceptive reality, "frustration grew at the inability to locate the enemy or identify him: How do you tell the enemy from the people?" (*TNL*, p. 229).

The resounding answer given by the narrators is that it is simply impossible. This answer legitimated a world view that asserted and condoned the inevitability of killing innocent Vietnamese. The simplest and most common formulation of this belief is expressed in the admonition given to soldiers new "incountry": "Look twice and you're dead" (*FF*, p. 99). A somewhat more apologetic tone marked the words of one veteran who insisted, "You can't tell who's your enemy. You got to shoot kids. You got to shoot women. You don't want to. You may be sorry that you did. But you might be sorrier if you didn't. That's the damn truth" (*N*, p. 213). Still another recounted how hesitation in taking a life could well result in a fatality—oneself: "I saw American kids . . . they were having a lot of trouble killing people, basically. I saw some fairly sensitive kids begin to know themselves because of this and begin to discover contradictions in their own thinking. And unfortunately this cost some of them their lives, because the minute they began to think they would move just a little less quickly under orders and pause just a little bit more before shooting at somebody" (*EWH*, p. 71).

Because, said one, "in this type of fighting it was impossible to know who the enemy was at any one time" (*EWH*, p. 69), all Vietnamese were immediately suspect. This fact of the enemy's invisibility is neatly captured in the soldier's linguistic habits:

"I noticed you called them gooks. I thought that would be what we called the enemy. Does everybody call them gooks?"

"We do around here, sir." He was enjoying his status as teacher. "Different units got different names for them, but it don't make no difference what you call them, you know. Friendly or not, they're all called the same" (*TKZ*, p. 18).

Obviously, a sensitivity to enthnosemantics isn't necessary to instantly recognize that a vocabulary that employs the same signifier to denote both friend and enemy reflects a fundamentally inchoate reality.

"Gooks," as an all-purpose term to identify any Oriental (including, ironically, the Americans' equally bewildered allies from the Republic of Korea), proved versatile because distinctions that appeared valid one moment could be refuted the next—in the time it takes to drop a hoe and grab a rifle. This use of the term "gook" nicely illustrates the GI's cognitive confusion: "There were gooks on the [perimeter] wire that night. It was regular gooks, VC, local people. They your friend during the day, but at night they Vietcong" (*N*, p. 82). The differences between "regular" gooks, "local" gooks, "foreign" (North Vietnamese) gooks, hostile gooks, and so on are open to sudden and unpredictable permutation and therefore cannot serve as sound premises upon which to base judgment and action.

This assessment was as true of aggregates as it was of individuals. The hamlet, as the basic unit of Vietnamese society, was often as tightly knit a social institution as the family in Western cultures, demonstrating the same commonality of purpose. Thus, a whole village could be VC. Americans, expecting to be met with cheering and kisses as a result of their initiation, might instead be greeted with a deadly hail of small arms fire. The one certainty in Vietnam was uncertainty: it was impossible to know which response they would receive until they actually entered the ville. As one soldier remarks, "In the center of this bastion lay a little droll Vietnamese village of thirty-two hundred souls, many of whom, most of whom, all of whom, who knows? were communists, some so dedicated red as to slip through the dark forest shooting American soldiers in their backs. A month ago they'd killed another lieutenant colonel. A weird war" (*M*, p. 99).

Adding to the uncertainty was the GIs' terror of child-assassins, a subject we have discussed in connection with the soldiers' initiation. If the basic training stories with which the soldiers were harangued seemed blood-curdling at home, they took on added urgency (and clinical detail) in the war zone. Once in Vietnam, the Americans continuously heard of, if not saw, the exploits of this most feared and monstrous manifestation of the invisible enemy.

The VC did, in fact, frequently use small children as human bombs. Almost nothing could be done to defend against this weapon and therefore it proved particularly nightmarish and effective. "Most of the GIs were suckers for little kids. They'd always pick them up. We had a little boy that was boobytrapped. He was about five years old. Somebody had put a bomb on him and sent him into a bar where there were a lot of GIs hanging out. Someone picked him up and he exploded. It killed five GIs" (*N*, p. 158). "Some Marines drop piaster notes and coins into the sea of hands holding up bottles of Coca-Cola; but they do not accept the sodas. In this Alice in Wonderland war, Coke is a weapon. The VC sometimes poison it or put ground glass in it and give it to the children to sell to Americans" (*RW*, p. 101); "A lot of GIs were booby-trapped by children throwing hand grenades at them. Who was the enemy? Anybody was fair game if you were in a contested area" (*N*, p. 316). As one soldier summed up the consensus on the most psychologically devastating weapon in the invisible enemy's arsenal, "Those little babysans are devils, man. No shit. Devils" (*FF*, p. 91). The enemy's almost preternatural invisibility, coupled with his non-human status as the Oriental other, combined to render each contact a terrifying encounter with beings of seemingly awesome powers. "Devils," "phantoms," "apparitions," and "ghosts" are terms commonly invoked by Americans to describe their foe.

Fields of Fire, discussed earlier in the section entitled "Fathers and Sons," dramatizes the meaning-wrenching quality of a brush with the invisible enemy. A member of Lt. Hodges' platoon, an ex-Harvard musician named Goodrich, finds the slaughter of seemingly innocent civilians so morally repugnant he refuses to shoot a fleeing figure wearing a ponytail, believing it to be a young woman. Goodrich's squad leader guns down the running "girl" and discovers that the ponytail is glued to the escapee's hat. The male corpse, moreover, is replete with a bandolier of ammunition strapped across his chest.

Later, Goodrich, no wiser in the ways of the invisible enemy, yanks a rifle out of the hands of one of his squad who is aiming at a Vietnamese child. Goodrich's reaction results in the soldier's instant death when the child drops into a ditch allowing the sniper behind the youngster to open fire. In the ensuing fire-fight, Goodrich loses a leg, and a number of his squad become casualties. Goodrich's intelligence and moral sensibility, although enviable traits in "the World," are a positive liability in "the Nam." The chaotic and deceptive environment demands instinctive reactions more than any sensitivity to ambiguity. "Look twice and you're dead" served as a fitting epitaph for the invisible enemy's victims.

Finally, the GIs' psychological misery was intensified by the enemy's intimate knowledge of the terrain. This knowledge enabled the VC to elude detection and pursuit. When the U. S. Forces mounted operations with their South Vietnamese counterparts, the VC simply disappeared into the jungle until the hunters gave up. The enemy broke off combat engagements as easily as they initiated them. "And then instead of really ending, the battle vanished. The North Vietnamese collected up their gear and most of their dead and 'disappeared' during the night, leaving a few bodies behind for our troops to kick and count" (*D*, p. 24).

Vietnam was perfectly suited to the needs of an insurgent guerilla force. The majority of the land was uninhabited and presumed uninhabitable—a perfect situation for playing a lethal game of hide-and-seek.[21] Places with forbidding-sounding names like "the Rockpile," the "Iron Triangle" and "the Parrot's Beak" provided sanctuary for the invisible enemy. Within the impenetrable three-tiered jungles, the VC and NVA were safe from observation and attack. To track them into their strongholds required superhuman fortitude, and the results were often negligible. One soldier remembers:

Once, I led a difficult platoon-sized patrol near Charlie Ridge. I like to think of it whenever I hear some general who spent his tour looking at maps and flitting around in helicopters claim that we could have won the war. First we had to hack our way through a patch of bamboo and elephant grass ten feet high, the worst, thickest patch of jungle we had encountered. Working in shifts, the point man and I chopped at the growth with a machete. When we had cut as much as we could, three or four marines would come up and flatten the wall of brush by hurling their bodies against it. That done, the rest of the platoon would move forward a few yards. Then the point man and I would start out again. All this in bake-oven heat. Coming out of the jungle, we entered a swamp, which we had to cross by hopping from one small island of solid ground to the next. Corporal Mixon lost his footing once, fell into a quicksand pool, and had sunk up to his chest before he was hauled out covered with muck and leeches. . . . The only trail up the ridge was an overgrown game-track. It was easy at first, but then the slope became so steep we had to climb hand over hand, clutching at the bone-gray roots of mahogany trees, hand over hand a foot at a time, gasping and sweating in the moist air. Sometimes a man fell, toppling several of those behind him as he rolled downhill. Thorn bushes clawed us, cordlike "wait-a-minute" vines coiled around our arms, rifles, and canteen tops with a tenacity that seemed almost human. When we finally reached the crest, I checked my map and watch: in 5 hours, and without making a single enemy contact, we had covered a little over half a mile (*RW*, pp. 138–39).

Although some American units did eventually become proficient at jungle warfare,[22] the advantage was almost always with the guerillas. The majority of these joint operations were hopelessly inadequate to the task of finding and destroying small bands of highly mobile, heavily armed insurgents capable of living off the land. Typically, such operations consisted of "invading" a contested area (à la WWII) with battalion-size units. The troops would then blunder around in the bush detonating booby traps left by an enemy who had long since vanished. As soon as the allies had departed, evacuating

their wounded and dead who had "found" the invisible enemy's handiwork, the VC and NVA would return to reestab-
lish control. One U. S. Marine describes the outcome of such
a formidable waste of men and munitions: "Operation Blast
Out began and ended in early August. Three thousand marines and ARVN soldiers, supported by tanks, artillery, planes,
and the six-inch guns of a U. S. Navy cruiser, managed to kill
two dozen Viet Cong in three days" (*RW*, p. 193). Even the
commander of MACV, General William Westmoreland, con-
ceded that these "sweeping operations" (or "reconnaissance in
force" as he preferred they be called) "failed to find the enemy
. . . so that many looked on search and destroy as aimless and
unrewarding. The U. S. military strategy employed in Vietnam, dictated by political decisions, was essentially that of a
war of attrition."[23]

Thus the American GI, prepared by a lifetime of cultural indoctrination to fight a conventional war, found himself in a
formless war chasing an invisible enemy. In this situation, the
meanings traditionally attached to war—heroism, nobility,
sacrifice, victory, duty, honor—became de-objectivated. Reality was simply no longer navigable using the old cognitive maps.
Soldiers in "the Nam" perceived themselves adrift in an alien
universe in which the familiar cognitive and normative land-
marks had disappeared. In the absence of these taken-for-
granted coordinates of experience (what sociologist Erving
Goffman calls "a basic reality kit"), the terrified soldiers were
presented with only one objective imposing a semblance of design on their frustrating, uncertain, dangerous, and primitive
existence: "Simply to kill: to kill Communists and to kill as
many of them as possible. Stack 'em like cordwood" (*RW*, p. xix).
The soldiers clung to this meaning-making and meaning-sus-
taining injunction with all the considerable desperation at their
disposal. One result of this confluence of people, policy, and
priorities was a war in which "we began to make a habit of
atrocities" (*RW*, p. 216). It is at that aspect of the Vietnam War
which we must now look.

The Barbarian Loosed

They go wild, Lieutenant. And there's nothing you can do about it. You'll go wild, too. Wild as hell. You spend a month in the bush and you're not a Marine anymore. Hell, you're not even a goddamned person. There's no tents, no barbed wire, no hot food, no jeeps or trucks, no clean clothes. Nothing. You're an animal.

—*Fields of Fire*, p. 68

One must understand that it's very easy to slip into a primitive state of mind, particularly if your life is in danger and you can't trust anyone.

—*Everything We Had*, p. 69

Before you leave here, sir, you're going to learn that one of the most brutal things in the world is your average nineteen-year-old American boy."

—*A Rumor of War*, p. 129

The preceding chapter, "Initiation," explained how the United States military served to de-objectivate meanings from civilian society affirming the sanctity of human life. The basic training regimen systematically discredited the idea of the integrity and inviolability of the individual. The civilized ideal was replaced by a military objectivation asserting the desirability of killing effectively, efficiently, and on command. The result was a world view glorifying the deliberate taking of human life—what we called "praying for war." Furthermore, the military levied on the image of the Oriental other as a fit object of the "pray for war" mentality by insisting on the Oriental's non-human stature.

In this chapter, the reality that these beliefs about human life and about the Oriental race in particular confronted in Vietnam has been analyzed. The distinctively contingent nature of experience in the war zone set the stage for especially horrifying events. The results of this unhappy conjunction of a world view denigrating the value of life with a world in which taking lives receives the highest priority are predictable. In short, the retreat from meaning led, inexorably, to the commission of atrocities.

The wholly novel aspects of the Vietnam War—its formlessness and the invisibility of the enemy—prompted one commentator to conclude that "the war in Vietnam is in many respects unprecedented in the extent to which its over-all strategy encourages brutality. Counter-insurgency warfare requires too hasty a judgment. A pajama-clad civilian cannot be distinguished from a similarly-clad insurgent in the time it takes the round to leave the barrel and strike its target" (*CWA*, p. 11). This brutality was exacerbated by the unusual political and geographic characteristics of the conflict in Southeast Asia. One soldier recognized how "the conflict in Vietnam combined the two most bitter forms of warfare, civil war and revolution, to which was added the ferocity of jungle war" (*RW*, p. xviii). The picture that emerges from the accounts is one of awesome and relentless blood-letting in which no one is spared. Such a situation, which we have designated "the barbarian loosed," demands elucidation.

The most obvious explanation for the occurrence of atrocities is the reliance on the body count as the sole measure of military effectiveness. Because "the measures of a unit's performance in Vietnam were not the distances it had advanced or the number of victories it had won" (*RW*, p. 160), the body count assumed primary importance. The emphasis on the body count implied a world view in which destroying human life meant only the substitution of a numerical value for a variable in an equation. In fact, the daily ritual of publicly posting both sides' losses in rear areas rendered death only statistically meaningful to the upper-echelon officers who designed operations. Because "victory was a high body-count, defeat a low kill-ratio, war a matter of arithmetic" (*RW*, p. xix), human suffering as a non-quantifiable phenomenon simply didn't exist.

The body count was often viewed as an end in itself, rather than as an approximation of an otherwise intangible goal. This confusion over ends and means caused one reporter to say: "Not that you didn't hear some over-ripe bullshit about it: Hearts and Minds, People of the Republic, tumbling dominoes, main-

taining the equilibrium of the Ding-dong by containing the ever
encroaching Doodah; you could also hear the other, some young
soldier speaking in all bloody innocence, saying 'All that's just
a *load*, man. We're here to kill gooks. Period' " (*D*, p. 20).

This fixation with numbers made the war-as-lethal-sport
ethos plausible. War became a contest in which dead bodies
were simply points to be tallied. In most units, soldiers contributing to the body count were credited with a "confirmed
kill" and rewarded according to an unofficial schedule:

Sometimes there were contests for the troops which were based on
points to be won and points that could be taken away. Points will be
awarded for the following:

   5—per man per day above 25 on an operation
  10—each possible body-count
  10—each 100 lbs. of rice
  15—each 100 lbs. of salt
  20—each mortar round
  50—each individual enemy weapon captured
 100—each enemy crew-served weapon captured
 100—each enemy body-count
 200—each tactical radio captured
 500—each individual weapon captured
 500—perfect score on CMMI (inspection)
1000—each prisoner of war

Points will be deducted for the following:

  50—each U. S. WIA (wounded in action)
 500—each U. S. KIA (killed in action) (*WL*, p. 65)

This kind of bounty system legitimated mercenary ruthlessness more than patriotic service. It made killing a matter of
personal profit and self-aggrandizement. Further, it conflated
quantity with success and ignored the distinction between the
dead *civilian* and the *enemy* corpse. (Obviously, no corpse can
protest his/her non-Communist sympathies.) Most importantly, the "confirmed kill" method of keeping score required
the soldier to submit proof of his claim. This requirement necessarily legitimated mutilation: a chunk of human anatomy was
considered incontrovertible proof of an enemy's demise. One
soldier ghoulishly recounts, "We had a thing in Nam. We used

to cut their ears off. If a guy had a necklace of ears he was a good killer, a good trooper. It was encouraged to cut ears off, to cut the nose off, to cut the guy's penis off. A female, you cut her breast off. It was encouraged to do these things. The officers expected you to do it or something was wrong with you" (*N*, p. 84). Another tells "about the colonel who had threatened to court-martial a spec 4 for refusing to cut the heart of a dead Viet Cong and feed it to a dog" (*D*, p. 204).

Tragically, these two accounts of official empowerment to commit outrages are not anomalous. Stories of vile excess abound throughout the narratives: "I had a friend that had a pet skull. He chopped the head off and he used to keep it in his tent" (*CWA*, p. 99); "We had this gook and we was gonna skin him . . . I mean he was already dead and everything, and the Lieutenant comes over and says, 'Hey asshole, there's a reporter in the TOC, you want him to come out and see that? I mean use your fucking heads, there's a time and place for everything. . . . " (*D*, p. 67); "A thing to do would be to cut the liver out and take a bite out of it and that would symbolize that the person would not go to Buddha heaven intact" (*EWH*, p. 219); "He used to carry a hatchet and he had it sharpened like a razor, and he'd sneak up on people that were coming up the bushes, and instead of taking them alive, he'd just cut their heads off, he'd put their heads in a bag and bring them back. It was in the First Division, and if you killed a certain number of the enemy you got a three-day pass, but you had to bring back their heads" (*CWA*, pp. 59–60). One correspondent, repeatedly witnessing this sort of barbarism, responded "Disgust doesn't begin to describe what they made me feel, they threw people out of helicopters, tied people up and put the dogs on them. Brutality was just a word in my mouth before that" (*D*, p. 67).

Simply put, the policy of equating a high body count with military success spawned a situation wherein atrocity was prescribed and rewarded. The United States military manipulated the definition of victory to generate new meanings bearing no relation to previously stipulated ones. This new meaning of military triumph—the number of enemy soldiers killed and the ratio of that number to our own casualties—

rendered obsolete the Geneva Convention. An unconventional war requiring an unconventional criterion of success legitimates a decidedly unconventional ethics. The retreat from the traditional meaning of victory authorized soldiers to "do things that seem not right now, but which seemed right at the time" (*N*, p. 94). One soldier said simply, "I discovered it's not difficult to kill a human being—in combat it's as instinctive as ducking bullets" (*COW*, p. 21).

Atrocity doesn't occur solely because of standing orders to amass a high body count. In the words of one noted anthropologist of war, A. F. C. Wallace, such orders must "not merely elicit a disciplined response but evoke a motivational system appropriate to the action to be taken" so that soldiers "will respond with anger, determination, fear, or whatever affective state is desired."[24] The affective state appropriate to the amassing of corpses was evoked by the reality of the GI's situation. The war was strategically incomprehensible, allowing for no resolution on the battlefield. It required the soldier to undergo another encounter with death, disfigurement, and humiliation daily at the hands of an enemy against whom there was virtually no chance to retaliate. "In war, where you're laying next to a guy you've been with eleven months and you're just like brothers, and all of a sudden his brains splattered all over your nose, that's a different type of harassment. And the worst part about it is, nine times out of ten when it happens the enemy will be gone. You can't even fire a shot. You can't take your anger out somewhere. You're left frustrated. That's harassment" (*EWH*, p. 101). Such utter torment, endured constantly for extended periods, could not long go unrequited. One platoon leader observed, "Some men could not withstand the stress of guerilla fighting: the hair-trigger alertness constantly demanded of them, the feeling that the enemy was everywhere, the inability to distinguish civilians from combatants created emotional pressures which built to such a point that a trivial provocation could make these men explode with the blind destructiveness of a mortar shell" (*RW*, p. xix).

It is these pressures, described concisely above, which induced the "motivational system" and "affective state" to which Wallace refers. The American soldier in Vietnam committed atrocities because the enemy remained unavailable as an object upon which to unleash violent energies. The soldier's rage found only one available outlet: the Vietnamese in whose name he was undergoing such torture. One soldier defiantly exclaimed, "I burn because I hate. I hate because I'm here. I hate every house, every tree, every pile of straw and when I see it I want to burn it" (*M*, p. 167). Another describes his rage as cumulative: "And then, after the longer you stayed there, the more you got to hate them, and the more you got to hate them, the more you'd take advantage of them, and you just start beating people up for no reason, and, say, you'd go through a village and you'd shoot a couple of shots, you know, in somebody's living quarters, and like nobody cared. And you became sicker and sicker every day" (*CWA*, p. 99). Still another, more eloquently, confesses to listening for the voice of the barbarian within and attending to its lethal urgings: "Finally, there was a hatred, a hatred buried so deep that I could not then admit its existence. I can now, though it is still painful. I burned with a hatred for the Viet Cong and with an emotion that dwells in most of us, one closer to the surface than we care to admit: a desire for retribution. . . . Revenge was one of the reasons I volunteered for a line company. I wanted a chance to kill somebody" (*RW*, p. 219).

This all-consuming hatred, coupled with direct orders to kill as many Communists as possible in a place where anybody might just be one, had consequences that were no less tragic for being predictable. As America's longest war seemed to drag on interminably, "the fighting had not only become more intense, but more vicious. Both we and the Viet Cong began to make a habit of atrocities" (*RW*, p. 216).

Many of the crimes against humanity committed by American troops involved prisoners of war. Understandably, the presence of the invisible enemy in human, tangible form unleashed a flood of emotion. Here, at last, was the dread Vietcong. No longer an evaporating shadow leaving a wake of all-too-palpable surprises, this flesh-and-blood soldier could now be made to suffer as the GI had. These prisoners (and suspects) were subjected to the full range of brutality by Americans, from summary execution to the most ingenious and painful torture: "No. I couldn't honestly believe that a man, especially an American—I don't think that Americans—I didn't think at that time that an American was capable, was capable of malicious, sadistic torture. A new guy who just arrived there got sick to his stomach when he saw these things. After a while it doesn't bother you. Some of them actually enjoyed it" (CWA, p. 55). "And the prisoner was hog-tied. I mean his hands and feet bound together. Then he proceeded to hit him on the head as hard as he could with the stock of an M–79 grenade launcher. After kicking him a couple of times, he finally walked off screaming obscenities" (CWA, p. 160). It is not necessary to recount here all the incidents of torture and murder recounted in the Vietnam War narratives. The "Bell Telephone Hour" as the favored method of interrogation employed by U. S. intelligence officers has already been discussed. After the Tet Offensive of 1968, a policy of immediately executing prisoners was in effect in many ground units, even though this practice led to a loss of potentially valuable intelligence data.[25] One combatant invokes the barbarian loosed as unique to the Vietnam conflict: "There is also the aspect of the Vietnam War that distinguished it from other American conflicts—its absolute savagery. I mean the savagery that promoted so many American fighting men—the good, solid kids from Iowa farms— to kill civilians and prisoners" (RW, p. xvii).

The stories of malicious abuse of prisoners of war and suspected Vietcong form a stomach-turning litany within the Vietnam corpus. Yet, such barbaric treatment can be rationalized, in part, by understanding the situation: an overwrought GI finally facing his nemesis. One soldier remembered that "the day after the one on which his squad was ambushed and half its members were wounded, several enemy prisoners were taken, and, in retaliation, two were summarily killed, 'to serve as an example.' A corporal who was still enraged over the ambush tried to strangle another of the prisoners; he had knotted a pancho nooselike, around the captive's neck and tightened it when a merciful lieutenant commanded him to desist" (COW, pp. 18–19). Very likely the sullen prisoner *was* the same man who, from his hiding place, detonated the mine that decimated one's squad. In any case, it was

hardly inconceivable. No such tentative strategy of exculpa-
tion pertains to those soldiers engaging in atrocities against
helpless villagers.

Since the widely publicized revelations concerning the
slaughter of 128 civilians in the hamlet-complex of My Lai 4,
no single feature of the Vietnam War has aroused more confusion or generated as much debate.[26] The specific events of
March 16, 1968—the My Lai massacre—are too familiar to be
recounted here. What does demand attention is the soldiers'
insistence that such wholesale slaughter occurred routinely
under the conditions that pertained in the war zone. Moreover, these atrocities were ordered by their superiors and subsequently covered up as a matter of policy. In the words of one
soldier, charged with the murder of a Vietnamese civilian,
"Whether committed in the name of principles or out of vengeance, atrocities were as common to the Vietnamese battlefields as shell craters and barbed wire" (*RW*, p. xviii).

The narrators illuminate the world view of the American
grunt by identifying and elaborating on the social processes
which make possible such behavior. In effect, they describe an
environment in which the usual forms of social control have
been swept aside. One soldier remarked, "It's weird, isn't it,
what you do, the things you do. You know, if I thought of a
child dying that's the way it was. That's war. Children die. You
kill them, they kill you. Women kill you, you kill them. That's
it. There's no Geneva Convention. There's no rules. There's
nothing" (*EWH*, p. 143). Clearly, ethical systems are also socially constructed objectivations maintained through plausibility structures, in this instance mechanisms of social control. As these mechanisms break down, so, too, do the ethical
considerations they legitimate. One soldier described the situation succinctly, "You had the license to do whatever you
wanted" (*N*, p. 94). Another, when queried about his reasons
for shooting an elderly woman, replied, "Just for the hell of it.
You can do anything there" (*CWA*, p. 93). A third demon-
strates a keen sociological understanding of his comrades' reactions to the abolition of social controls: "And so the hate goes
out, the hate goes out against them all, it doesn't matter who
they are . . . they all of a sudden find themselves with the

power of life and death in their hands, and they have never had this power before. I mean they just get out of high school and all of a sudden they have all this power, and it does something to them. Plus I don't think they have anything in the way of real moral strength by the time they get over there. Some do, quite a few of the older ones do, but most of the average guys you know, they haven't considered what they are doing. . . . They just go. It's the thing to do. They were told to go and they go" (*CWA*, p. 179). For many, counter-guerilla warfare meant "working in remote places under little direct authority, acting out their fantasies with more freedom than most men ever know" (*D*, p. 50). As one inhabitant of this ethically unobstructed universe said, "You begin to understand how genocide takes place" (*N*, p. 154).

Of course, not all American combat troops massacred civilians. Said one, "Marine training had not completely erased the years we had spent at home, at school, in church, learning that human life was precious and the taking of it wrong" (*RW*, p. 117). But for others, caught in "a time and place for thousands of men to play for keeps" (*COW*, p. 76), loosing the barbarian made its own perverse sense. The confusion they experienced was so profound that "they did not know how to feel when they saw villages burning. Revenge? Peace of mind or anguish? They did not know. They did not know good from evil" (*GAC*, p. 273). For these men, in the words of one of them, "taking a life was nothing. It was customary" (*N*, p. 84).

It is clearly beyond the scope of the present study to adjudicate the GIs' innocence or guilt. When search and destroy missions were in actuality pillage and massacre exercises and soldiers received direct orders to kill anything that moved in a "free-fire zone," the line between duty and barbarism is a fine one. One soldier said, "I saw cruelty and brutality that I didn't expect to see from our own people against the villagers. It took me a while incountry to realize why it was happening" (*EWH*, p. 69). Another testifies: "You'd be in a hamlet and a guy would say, 'Hey man, shoot that son of a bitch over there.' The guy would turn around and fire an M–16 into his chest. Wiped out. It was a farmer—didn't have no gun. That's common—knock off a civilian for the hell of it" (*CWA*, p. 76).

The narrators argue that these were not men who, under other circumstances, would have willed "the barbarian loosed." Only in the pressure cooker of Vietnam would they ever "execute civilians for the sheer joy of shooting at running objects" (*EWH*, p. 54). As one of them notes, "I know a lot of guys who were nice guys back in the States, but Vietnam changed them. Some of them were really shy cats back in the States, but after two or three months in Vietnam they were just killers. They didn't even know who they were. They were completely different people" (*CWA*, p. 65). A seasoned major summed this up nicely when he told a lieutenant new "incountry": "I just look at you and say, 'That used to be me. But it isn't anymore' " (*FF*, p. 70).

The official U. S. policy regarding the killing of what the military called "non-hostile indigenous personnel" may best be described as "malign neglect." As one foot soldier commented, "It got fucked up when they made it as easy for us to shoot as not to shoot" (*D*, p. 61). Large areas of the countryside were under "loose policy," leaving it a matter of individual discretion whether or not the people in that area were to be considered hostile and shot on sight. Certainly, no soldier reports being reprimanded for not exercising restraint ("fire-discipline" in military jargon), at least not until some aggrieved hamlet chief registered a complaint with Saigon. Virtually all the GIs agree that "killing is the easiest part of the whole thing. Sweating twenty-four hours a day, seeing guys drop all around you of heat-stroke, not having food, not having water, sleeping only three hours a night for weeks at a time, that's what war is" (*N*, p. 97). It is not surprising that under such inhumane conditions, inhumane beliefs flourish. Compassion is simply a luxury in a world of "dead people, guts in the goddamn dirt, miserable civilians" (*FF*, p. 68). As one observer concluded about the vengeance wreaked by "the barbarian loosed": "There's one thing that stands out about these particular offenses. . . . They did not occur in the United States. Indeed, there are some that would say that they did not even occur in civilization, when you are out on combat operations" (*COW*, p. 102).

Again, sociological understanding implies neither apologetic nor condemnation. If the argument here suggests sympathy for the soldiers, it is only to *do justice to*, not *pass judgment upon*, them. Such an argument is based upon an appreciation of the human need for a meaningful symbolic universe in which to live. Even the most perverse behavior emanates from the struggle to give coherence to the world. Such coherence is, given man's innate sociality, a collective product built upon legitimating theories. It is to the reconstitution of a coherent symbolic universe and the legitimations it engendered that we now turn.

Survival

What had begun as an adventurous expedition had turned into an exhausting, indecisive war of attrition in which we fought for no cause other than our own survival.

—*A Rumor of War*, p. xiv

At the nitty-gritty it was only survival. It was only to come home and see your friends, your family, not to shame them, not to hurt them. Come back to America. And it wasn't like "America the great, the land of the beautiful." I just wanted to come home.

—*Everything We Had*, p. 119

Shit, man, the trick of being in the Nam is getting *out* of the Nam. And I don't mean getting out in a plastic body bag. I mean getting out alive, so my girl can grab me so I know it.

—*If I Die in a Combat Zone*, p. 141

Our analysis of the disparity between WWII meanings and Vietnam War realities has disclosed how these meanings—glory, patriotism, honor, duty, victory, sacrifice, nobility—were tested and found wanting in Vietnam. The soldiers themselves describe the war as a massive exercise in de-objectivation: "That war shattered my whole image of the United States, of freedom and democracy, of the world we live in, all the ide-

als I had gone to Vietnam with. The sacrifice was a lie. The
war was a fraud. 'I pledge allegiance to the flag' just died" (*N*,
p. 310); "Then all my ideas about kill the enemy, patriotism,
gung-ho, that all went down the drain" (*CWA*, p. 121); "He was
the only member of the platoon who spoke consistently of national objectives, communism or winning a war. But even he
had recently ceased such speculations" (*FF*, p. 219); "Before I
went to Vietnam, my feelings were highly ambivalent. After I
got to Vietnam my feelings were strengthened against the war,
and I think I began to become even more disillusioned with
Americans over there for even more reasons than I had before
I went" (*CWA*, p. 205); "I began to realize the extent of the lie,
all the kinds of lies . . . I saw it with my own eyes constantly"
(*N*, p. 147). Perhaps this "retreat from meaning" was best expressed by a member of traditionally the proudest branch of
the American Armed Services: "It just doesn't mean anything
to be a Marine anymore, Lieutenant. Vietnam did that" (*FF*,
p. 208).

One reporter, having covered the war for some half-dozen
years, observed that "most of the veterans began to change their
minds about U. S. involvement in Vietnam during their first
three months there" (*WL*, p. 332). Such a radical reinterpre-
tation resulted from the meaning-subverting predicament in
which they found themselves. One GI notes that "they had lost
some of their friends and most of their old convictions about
the reasons for the war . . . if you pointed to the casualty list
and asked them why their friends had died, they would not
have replied with some abstract speech about preserving democracy and stopping Communism. Their answer would have
been simple and concrete: 'Well, Jack was killed by a sniper
and a mortar got Bill and Jim stepped on a mine' " (*RW*, p. 205).

Clearly, the meanings which the soldiers brought with them
from home disintegrated in the war zone. However, humans
do not, indeed *cannot*, exist without meaning. Every situation
in which a human actor is present is an occasion for an interpretation of experience. As Peter Berger says, "All human
beings have meaning and seek to live in a meaningful world."[27]
This fact is given in man's basic constitution. Because consciousness "is always intentional; it always intends or is di-

rected toward objects," humans are continuously engaged in the process of re-cognizing (interpreting) meanings.[28] This process may, as in the case of Vietnam, involve rejecting one set of meanings and substituting an alternative meaning-complex for them.

This disposition to interpretation begs a crucial question: if the GIs shed the traditional WWII meanings in the course of their "retreat," what meanings did they then embrace to restore *nomos*? The answer is that the final repository of meaning and value became *sheer physical survival*, "breathing in and breathing out, some kind of choice all by itself" (*D*, p. 16). This haven of meaning, grounded in a bio-instinctual drive, kept chaos at bay by providing a basis for organizing behavior. In a sense, the soldiers were "thrown back" upon organismic, rather than cultural, knowledge for guidance.

The soldiers found in the imperative of survival a self-evident, "genetically-objectivated" meaning. As an immediate physical sensation, sheer being posed no problems of explanation or legitimation. Existence doesn't require an elaborate plausibility structure. Various thinkers have called such fundamentally self-evident facts "experience-near concepts" or "at hand" (therefore not subject to appropriation by initiation).[29] Simply, such facts are unselfconsciously meaningful to actors within a situation. Whatever terminological twist one prefers, existence and the value of its continuation is viewed as a *brute fact of experience*.

The implausibility of other objectivations made staying alive the only meaningful reality. As they eloquently attest: "The hardest thing to come to grips with is that making it through Vietnam—surviving—is probably the only worthwhile part of the experience. It wasn't going over there and saving the world from Communism or defending the country. The matter of survival was the only thing you could get any gratification from" (*N*, p. 315). "It was all he had thought about for months, the major topic of conversation in the bush. Life's goals reduced to ground zero: stay alive long enough to leave" (*FF*, p. 225). "I'm coming out alive, I promise—promise—the sacred words that Mason's invincible spirit gave to his vulnerable flesh: Mason's and each and every soldier's in M" (*M*, pp. 62–63).

"November would be spent in the jungle of the Central Highlands, where everything seemed impermanent and the only
thing of value to either side was survival" (*TZK*, p. 99). "For
their faces were not those of children, and their eyes had the
cold, dull expression of men who are chained to an existence
of ruthless practicalities. They struggled each day to keep dry,
to keep their skin from boiling up with jungle rot, and to stay
alive" (*RW*, p. 223). In the most succinct formulation, "There
are things and there are things, but your life is your life and
you try to save it. It ain't a laughing matter" (*N*, p. 171).

This perception of survival as the sole measure of meaning
and ultimate motivation for action helps to explain some of the
alarming features of the Vietnam War. One of these features
was the readiness of American soldiers to take lives indiscriminately. U. S. troops were ruthless in a way that contra-
dicted their identity as saviors of a defenseless people. However, they insist that virtually all of this bloodshed was part
of a desperate attempt to secure their own survival. In light
of the law of self-preservation, the "barbarian loosed" appears
less a vengeful demon and more a frantic mortal.

One battle-scarred veteran noted that his men "were made
pitiless by an overpowering greed for survival. Self-preservation, that most basic and tyrannical of all instincts, can turn
a man into a coward or, as was more often the case in Vietnam, into a creature who destroys without hesitation or remorse whatever poses even a potential threat to his life" (*RW*,
p. xix). Two comments on this brutality-as-safe-conduct-pass
perspective stand out: "I have to admit I enjoyed killing. It gave
me a great thrill while I was there. My attitude was, the less
of them there were, the better my chances of making it" (*N*,
p. 203); "Lieutenant, I've got a wife and two kids at home and
I'm going to see 'em again and don't care who I've got to kill
or how many of 'em to do it" (*RW*, p. xix).

The ultimate authority granted self-preservation explains the
unofficial truce observed by many line units. Cognizant of the
stalemate at the Paris Peace Talks, some outfits declared peace
by simply committing what the Uniform Code of Military Justice designates "dereliction of duty." Weary of being destroyed
in routine search-and-destroy operations, many outfits simply

stopped going out on patrol. More frequently than ever before in America's military history, U. S. troops did the unthinkable: they unilaterally withdrew from the war.[30] One says, "I was known as a definite survivor. I didn't chase Charlie that far after I left the helicopter. I didn't. I'm sorry, but I have to tell you the truth. One of the first things you realized when you got to Nam was that you weren't going to win this war. There was no way we could win doing what we were doing. After the first month me and everybody else over there said, 'I'm going to put in my twelve months and then I'm getting the fuck out of here. It's not worth it" (*N*, p. 122). Another recalls, "When it came to survival, we just avoided stuff. I didn't kick off ambushes when I could have. There was no reason to. Killing them meant nothing. It was just stupid. I mean, they saw us walk past them during the day and they could walk past us at night. I walked in a very distinctive formation. The VC knew who I was and if they didn't shoot at me during the day, I wouldn't shoot at them at night. We just survived" (*EWH*, p. 127). Another tells how "We refused to cross the river. 'Look, this isn't worth it. They don't bother us and we don't bother them.' And it was a great way of living. Survival, right?" (*EWH*, p. 116).

Even when American troops didn't strike a tacit bargain with the enemy, they often conducted their war with a notable lack of zeal. In marked contrast to the spirit of his "do-or-die" initiation, one GI remarked, "I began to realize months later that we were the war. If we wanted to go out and chase people around and shoot at them and get them to shoot back at us, we had a war going on. If we didn't do that, they left us alone. After a while it became clear that there was a pattern here. Our people, including Special Forces, used to stop at four-thirty and have a happy hour and get drunk. There was no war after four-thirty. On Saturdays, no war. On Sundays, no war. On holidays, no war. That's right, a nine-to-five war" (*EWH*, p. 5). Another reminisced, "When we would have a NVA shiper who was a fucking bad shot we would leave him alone. If we killed him, they might replace him with a man who could really shoot. Better to have this dude who couldn't hit a barn. We loved the bad ones. He'd fire and all of a sudden you'd see a cow fall down a few yards away. The schmuck" (*N*, p. 120). Clearly, survival had replaced duty to country as the highest priority.

In a situation like this, where survival takes precedence over all other objectives, traditional allegiances will inevitably shift. For many Americans, especially veterans of the Paradigm War, the most horrifying aspect of the Vietnam War was "officer-cide," what the enlisted men called "fragging." Fragging refers to the disabling, usually by hand grenade, of a superior officer felt to be especially inept. If a particular leader jeopardized his troops unnecessarily or callously dismissed the numbers of casualties they sustained, he would be a prime candidate for fragging. The narrators insist that every incident of this sort of which they are personally aware was a response to a superior's lethal fatuousness. Fragging was thus a means of meting out "people's justice" and safeguarding the soldiers' own lives. One soldier, "remembering the stories from Basic School . . . understood immediately why an individual would want to wound an incompetent officer with a grenade. It's not vin-dictiveness. . . . It's self-preservation" (*FF*, p. 80).

Fragging, although perturbing, is simply a lurid manifes-tation of a larger issue: the de-objectivation of military mean-ings, in this instance discipline. Equally revealing in this con-text, and much more widespread than fragging, was the soldiers' refusals to obey direct, lawful orders that exposed them to peril. During the final years of the war, GIs maintained that disobeying such orders was their "duty"—to themselves and their comrades. As a result, the military's pride in preserving the value of discipline in an otherwise self-indulgent society took a severe beating in Vietnam. One officer said of his sub-ordinates, "they were . . . the kind who would say *no*. . . . They simply emanated a weird sort of stubbornness, not really hostile, perhaps not even conscious of their part. Like they've all been beat and one more *fuck you* to some mindless order isn't gonna sink them any deeper, and they know it" (*FF*, p. 74). If it became apparent that the VC were amenable to a tacit peace treaty but one's commanding officer posed a constant threat to life and limb, the designation "enemy" attached it-self to the latter.

The soldiers stipulate that they never conceived of their actions as a "mutiny" or "rebellion" as those terms are defined in the Uniform Code of Military Justice. Their refusals were limited to those instances where their personal safety was at stake. Although they "saw the officers not as courageous men making lonely decisions, but as men willing to accept pettiness, untruths, a rigid and relentless pecking order, and even glad to do it" (*WL*, p. 251), their actions were not intended as an assault on the military hierarchy as such. They insist that all they desired was *to stay alive*—and that such a goal often meant refusing to commit suicide-by-duty. One anecdote suggests the character of such breaches of discipline:

We had this lieutenant, honest to Christ he was about the biggest dip-shit fool of all time, all time. We called him Lieutenant Gladly 'cause he was always going like, "Men . . . Men, I won't never ask you to do nothing I wouldn't do myself gladly," what an asshole. We was on 1338 and he goes to me, "Take a little run up the ridge and report to me," and I goes like, "Never happen, Sir." So he goes up there himself and damned if the fucker didn't get zapped. He said we was gonna have a real serious talk when he come back, too. Sorry 'bout that (*D*, p. 26).

One of the structural features of the Vietnam War contributing to this survival mentality was the arbitrary time limit imposed on the soldier's stay in the war zone. Survival was a tangible goal because the rotation system mandated a single twelve or thirteen month tour of duty. Unlike WWII, in which one served "for the duration," in Vietnam "no one ever talked about when-this-lousy-war-is-over. Only 'How much time you got?' " (*D*, p. 118). As one reporter noted, "The soldiers had a year in Vietnam, sometimes a little less. Over and over they counted each day gone and all the days left to get through. They counted all the time and told you fifty days were left, ten days, three days. The Army counted everything else, insisted that all things be counted, until the numbers meant nothing, but still the counting kept on" (*WL*, p. 65). The parallel between the body count and the day count made war a quantifiable endeavor for all. The tour of duty, like the body count, conflated quantity with efficacy. In the words of one soldier,

Toward the end of my tour, when I started knowing what I was doing in the jungle and started knowing what to do under fire, it was just about time to go home. If that happened to me—if I was just getting good in the jungle and really knew what to do and I was going home— what good is it? I'm going to be replaced by a guy who is as green as I was when I got here, and by the time he is good at it he's going to be replaced by a guy who is green. It's no wonder we never got a foot-hold in the place (*EWH*, p. 43).

Another warrior wrote, "Time was everything. Time kept them there and time would let them leave. They were doing time, marking off the days, keeping track religiously of exactly how long it would be before thirteen months were up and the in-sanity ended" (*FF*, p. 213). Under such ironclad time con-straints, lofty ideals paled when contrasted with the ghastly prospect of departing Vietnam via "the KIA Travel Bureau" (*D*, p. 23).

For example, the most massively objectivated among these ideals was manhood. In civilian as well as military life, man-hood was viewed as sacred. In America, males learned to re-gard death as preferable to relinquishing the social identity of "man." In Vietnam, however, this meaning lost the power to shape behavior when compared to the privileged meaning in-vested in survival. As one soldier testifies, "That's like I was wounded three times and I don't have a purple heart. Nobody gets a purple heart. It's chicken to get a purple heart. But it was about this time that we discovered that three purple hearts gets you sent home. That's when everybody changed their minds about purple hearts" (*EWH*, p. 31). The stigma at-tached to the identity of "chicken" or "coward," previously per-ceived as unbearable, became inconsequential in the hier-archy of meanings objectivated in Vietnam.

Although the "civilized" (and, in a sense, civilizing) mean-ings brought to Vietnam became de-objectivated there, forcing the GIs to rely on a biological drive to infuse experience with meaning, the forms of society did not cease to function. The soldier's cognitive trial-by-chaos confirms the basic presupposition of any philosophical anthropology worthy of the name: man is ineradicably a social being. Although the survival instinct is given in man's biological nature, *survival was, nonetheless, a social meaning*—shared by, and confirmed through interaction with, other men and entailing specifically social consequences. The world view of "survival as ultimate value" existed by virtue of the very same social processes as the world view it had replaced. Because "only the madman or the rare case of genius can inhabit a world of meaning all by himself,"[31] the meaning of survival had to be realized through social forms.

These social forms, the roles and institutions through which self-preservation was, if not mobilized, then channeled and expressed, allowed the soldiers to redefine reality, including their own identities, in meaningful ways. The retreat from meaning never inclined the men to perceive themselves as a mass of isolated individuals, "so many liquid molecules."[32] They didn't, in sociological terminology, experience anomie. Despite the disorder and low frequency of triviality (features conducive to anomic terror) the narrators report a puzzling absence of social disorganization.

A closer inspection of the "retreat from meaning" reveals that the specific meanings involved were those imposed by the large bureaucratic institutions of public life, especially the government and the media. The retreat was not to chaos, but to smaller, people-sized institutions that permitted face-to-face confirmation of existential meanings. In sociological terms, the soldiers withdrew sympathy and support from the "megastructures" that had been the primary determiners of meanings and transferred their allegiance to an informal Gemeinschaft social order. They invested moral authority in "mediating structures" which stand between the purely private sphere in all its anomic precariousness and the alienating megastructures whose credibility had collapsed in Vietnam.[33] These mediating structures—the squad, the platoon, the company[34]—served as the meaning-generating and meaning-maintaining apparatus of social process. They can be directly contrasted to the vast and remote megastructures like the Department of

Defense, the Office of the Presidency, and the Joint United States Public Affairs Office.

Social theorists have long recognized the efficacy of mediating structures in providing an interstitial zone, a "home," between the State on the one hand and the individual on the other. Edmund Burke's classic formulation is especially apposite: "To be attached to the subdivision, to love the little platoon we belong to in society, is the first principle (the germ as it were) of public affections."[35] Others contributing to an understanding and appreciation of the unique role played by mediating structures include Tocqueville, Marx, Toennies, Weber, Simmel, Veblen, and Nisbet—a virtual who's who of the sociological tradition. Durkheim, especially, emphasized the "little aggregations" sustaining social meanings as the foundations for social life.[36]

Self-preservation was rooted in human biology but was channeled in specific directions in the social matrix of mediating structures. Instead of the Armageddon of "the war of all against all," the battlefields of Vietnam played host to a Gemeinschaft world of mediating structures uniting individuals in common purpose.[37] As one soldier recalls, "Under fire the strangest kinds of camaraderie would develop. It had nothing whatever to do with patriotism. It did have a great deal to do with taking care of each other. Because when you're out there, the basic idea is to stay alive" (*EWH*, p. 72). Another insists that "each of us fought for himself and for the men beside him. The only way out of Vietnam, besides death or wounds, was to fight your way out. We fought to live. . . . It was . . . a war for survival . . . in which each soldier fought for his own life and the lives of the men beside him, not caring who he killed in that personal cause or how many or in what manner" (*RW*, pp. 235, 217). One veteran said simply, "We fight for each other. We're really tight here. Nobody else cares for us." This comment prompted his interviewer to remark, "They often spoke like this: in the killing zone, among their own, they were not lonely or selfish anymore" (*WL*, p. 67).

In the mediating structure, as in any institutional order, human activity was organized in mutually recognizable and predictable patterns—*in roles*. Role is a concept of central importance for sociology and social psychology. We will devote much attention to it in the next chapter. At this point, it is simply necessary to note that role-formation and role-assumption were important in restoring meaning and identity to the soldiers after they had effected their "retreat." Although the attenuation of some roles was inevitable in Vietnam, e.g., hero, patriot, savior, others remained intact. Of course, the military had already assigned roles to all members of the mediating structure. The most basic role distinction was between leader and follower, i.e., between officer and enlisted. The survival mentality, as we witnessed, devastated the traditional obligations legislated through these roles. Other roles depended upon the division of labor required by a large, bureaucratic conglomerate like the military. These roles, the MOS (Military Occupational Specialty), were vital to the maintenance of the mediating structure and its ostensible goal of group survival. For example, a platoon still required the services of a medic, a radio operator, a scout, a sniper, a machine-gunner, and so forth.

Yet the new meanings erected in Vietnam called for the creation of new roles. Behaviors generated by and organized around sheer survival-value became institutionalized in roles. For instance, one role constructed in Vietnam, to which an individual might be assigned on the basis of an extremely nonstandard aptitude test, was "fragger." When an officer or NCO had incurred his troops' wrath, it usually fell to one member of an outfit to dispose of the offending party. In *Fields of Fire*, a GI nicknamed Phony takes great pride in fulfilling the technical and motivational demands of his role:

Phony's face lit up. "Yeah. Well, [Sgt.] Austin has got to go. . . . "
Phony nodded his head judiciously, "Uh, huh. Well, I just gotta do *him*. . . . "
"Do Kersey. Do Austin. Do the Colonel. Do me if I piss you off. You cain' do everybody in the world, Phony."
Phony grinned mischievously, "Don't piss me off, Cannonball. . . . "

Phony held a grenade in his hand. He pulled the pin, then casually let the spoon fly, never losing his bland grin. He tossed it expertly, five meters on the other side of Austin. Austin started to rise. *Boom.* He fell on his face, motionless.
Phony yelled loudly, *"Corpsman up!"* (*FF*, pp. 130–31, 141)

Other Vietnam-specific roles include the "charmed grunt" (a soldier believed by his peers to have been blessed by Lady Luck), the "short-timer" (a GI whose tour is nearly completed and thus is unofficially exempted from hazardous assignment), and the "pogue" (a soldier with a desk job out of harm's way). These roles were formulated within the bounded social world of the Gemeinschaft mediating structure. By giving institutional support to the idea of survival, the platoon made self-preservation a social fact as well as a biological drive.

Mediating structures can be undermined or empowered by the megastructures under whose authority they fall. For instance, the Federal Government can impose constraints that render a neighborhood impotent in generating meanings that meet residents' needs. Government policies that dictate the economic, ethnic, or racial makeup of a particular neighborhood would be an example.[38] In Vietnam, the megastructure's policy of automatically rotating troops—the tour of duty—diminished the mediating structure's capacity to sustain feelings of solidarity.

A Gemeinschaft's ability to retain "public affections" depends upon its remaining relatively isolated and stable over time. A face-to-face social surrounding demands a degree of intimacy unattainable when the "faces" constituting it undergo frequent permutation. The tour of duty, in conjunction with the high incidence of combat casualties, imposed a ceiling upon the duration and intensity of that intimacy. One soldier, observing this erosion of "public affections," said, "Later in the war that sort of feeling became rarer in infantry battalions. Men were killed, evacuated with wounds, or rotated home at a constant rate, then replaced by other men who were killed, evacuated, or rotated in their turn. By that time, a loss only meant a gap in the line that needed filling" (*RW*, p. 155). Another gave voice to this withering of fellowship by noting that "a dead buddy is some tough shit, but bringing your own ass out alive will sure help you get over it" (*D*, p. 26).

Obviously, as a social arrangement, mediating structures are not an unmixed blessing. The above quotations should serve to underline their fragility. Because mediating structures are institutionally "soft," they are relatively unreliable. In addition, mediating structures tend to foster parochialism. The virtues of smallness and proximity entail the liability of promoting indifference to larger issues whose effects cannot be immediately assessed. For instance, one of the most common phrases in the GI's vocabulary in Vietnam was "Somebody Else's War." This phrase described any contact in which the speaker and his listeners weren't directly involved. Two soldiers, from their vantage point atop a ridge, illustrate this parochialism:

Hodges could hear the firefight in the distance. First platoon was perhaps a mile and a half away. There were high stacattos [sic] of AK–47s, punctuated by the boom of B–40 rockets. M–16s and LAAWs returned fire. He sat, listening alertly while monitoring Rock Man and Captain Crazy on the net.

Snake approached from the perimeter's edge, looking toward the village where the first platoon was fighting. "They are in the shit *again*. Get some, first platoon. . . . "

Hodges lit a cigarette, agreeing. "There it is, Snake. Now when they get inside that ville, they're gonna burn it down. And we'll go through there tomorrow on the way to Chau Phongs and we'll hit us a booby trap, thanks to first platoon.

Then he lit Snake's smoke, and they watched the rest of Someone Else's War a mile away. (*FF*, pp. 170–71).

Indeed, the war often seemed to be waged between different branches of the Armed Services (or different units within one branch), rather than between those branches and the North Vietnamese Army. The traditional hostility between the U. S. Army and the U. S. Marine Corps escalated uncontrollably during the Vietnam War.[39] "And when the Cav[alry Division] sent an outfit to relieve the Marines on 471, it killed off one of the last surviving romances about war left over from the movies: there was no shouting, no hard kidding, no gleeful obscenities, or the old, 'Hey, where you from? Brooklyn? No kidding! Me too!' The departing and arriving files passed one another without a single word being spoken" (*D*, p. 158). Within the Army, the feud between the airborne divisions and the infantry units became a private war. Paratroopers would refer to infantrymen as "legs," a term carrying more opprobrium than can adequately be conveyed here. The ground-pounders held their beret-wearing brethren in equally low esteem. This antagonism frequently erupted in violent exchanges better suited to encounters with the official enemy.

Whether or not the mediating structures functioned smoothly and with positive, negative, or mixed results, one fact stands out: social forms continued to provide meaning and value for experience. Even though the meaning and value under consideration was instinctual in origin, it was through culture that the soldiers adapted to the existential pressures of the war zone. That adaptation involved modifying "historically created systems of meaning in terms of which they gave form, order, point, and direction to their lives."[40]

In the next chapter, we shall examine how this modified system of meaning withstood the rigors of homecoming. Our goal is to understand how the soldiers who survived to return to the United States physically intact perceived themselves, nonetheless, as "walking wounded."

<h2 style="text-align:center">NOTES</h2>

1. Peter Berger, *Facing Up to Modernity* (New York: Basic Books, 1977), p. 27.

2. Ibid., p. xii.

3. Ibid.

4. Ibid., p. 172.

5. Ibid., p. 107.

6. Peter Berger and Hansfried Kellner, *Sociology Re-Interpreted* (New York: Doubleday and Co., 1981), p. 74.

7. Berger, *Facing Up to Modernity*, p. 107.

8. The historiography of the Salem, Massachusetts, witchcraft "hysteria" (which term implies the scientific and rational categories typically employed to account for the events in question) nicely illustrates this aspect of belief systems. Attempts to explain the witchcraft "craze" range from the psychological [Marion Starkey, *The Devil In Massachusetts* (Garden City, N.Y.: Doubleday, 1949)] to the medical [Stanford Fox, *Science and Justice in Massachusetts Witchcraft Trials* (Baltimore: Hopkins Press, 1968)] to the sociological [Kai T. Erikson, *Wayward Puritans* (New York: Wiley and Sons, 1966)] to the socio-economic [Boyer and Nissenbaum, *Salem Possessed* (Cam-

bridge: Harvard University Press, 1974)] to the feminist [Selma Williams, *Riding the Nightmare* (New York: Atheneum, 1978)] to the pharmacological [Linda R. Caporal, "Ergotism: The Satan Loosed in Salem?" *Science*, April 2, 1976]. To the best of our knowledge, the only current interpretation that concedes the possible validity of the participants' understanding is C. Hansen, *Witchcraft at Salem* (New York: New American Library, 1969).

9. Berger, *Facing Up to Modernity*, p. 11.

10. Ibid., p. 173.

11. Peter Berger, *The Heretical Imperative* (New York: Doubleday and Co., 1979), p. 32.

12. Between 1961 and 1974 a total of 56,555 Americans died in Vietnam. Out of that total, 10,326 deaths were attributable to non-hostile causes. For a breakdown by year, see Gloria Emerson, *Winners and Losers* (New York: Random House, 1976), p. 58.

13. Some experts argue that it was not until the Arab-Israeli War of 1973 that some of the innovative weapons used routinely in Vietnam by American ground troops had been adequately tested under combat conditions. See General Donn A. Starry, *Armored Combat in Vietnam* (New York: Arno Press, 1980).

14. For a complete discussion of the major role played by aircraft in Vietnam, consult Colonel Dewey Waddell and Major Norm Wood, *Air War—Vietnam* (New York: Arno Press, 1978); and Ralph Littauer and Norman Uphoff, *The Air War in Indochina* (Boston: Beacon Press, 1972).

15. Berger, *Facing Up to Modernity*, p. xv.

16. Ibid.

17. George C. Herring, *America's Longest War: The United States and Vietnam, 1950–1975* (New York: John Wiley and Sons, 1979), p. 92.

18. David Halberstam, *The Best and the Brightest* (New York: Harper and Row, 1969).

19. Berger, *Facing Up to Modernity*, p. xvi.

20. Ibid., p. xvii.

21. Eighty percent of South Vietnam's 16 million people lived on less than 40 percent of the land, most of them along the coast and the fertile rice-growing region south of Saigon known as the Mekong Delta. This pattern left thousands of square miles of jungle and swamp in which the VC could erect elaborate staging areas, equivalent in some cases to U. S. base camps, which included hospitals, recreation facilities, training grounds, and ammunition depots. The vegetation provided natural cover which prevented these staging areas from detection by aircraft.

22. Several elite units were especially equipped and trained to fight a guerilla war. Because the VC operated primarily at night to avoid detection, these special units were required to develop a familiarity with the terrain equal to the opposition's. The U. S. Army LURPs (Long Range Reconnaissance Patrol), the U. S. Navy SEALs (Sea, Air, and Land), and U. S. Marine Force Recon (Reconnaissance) proved themselves adept at counterinsurgency warfare. (The U. S. Army Special Forces, by far the best known of these elite outfits, served in primarily a different capacity in Vietnam.) The effectiveness of these teams suggests that American soldiers were not somehow intrinsically incapable of beating the guerillas at their own game but rather were hampered by a military strategy which refused to acknowledge the realities of waging an unconventional war.

23. William C. Westmoreland, *A Soldier Reports* (New York: Doubleday and Co., 1976), pp. 152–53.

24. A. F. C. Wallace, "Psychological Preparations for War," in *War: The Anthropology of Armed Aggression*, ed. Morton Fried, Marvin Harris, and Robert Murphey (Garden City, N.Y.: The Natural History Press, 1968), p. 175.

25. Officially, the United States took 102,000 military prisoners of war. For obvious reasons, the number of prisoners captured and subsequently added to the body count cannot be determined.

26. The issue of what we, following the usage of the Vietnam narrators, call "atrocities" is exceedingly complex. Technically, such acts constitute the commission of "war crimes." For a thorough treatment of the legal aspects of such violations, including a comparison with Nazi brutalities, see Telford Taylor, *Nuremberg and Vietnam: An American Tragedy* (New York: Quadrangle Books, 1970). The philosophical issues raised by Taylor's analysis are considered in Richard Wasserstrom, "The Laws of War," in *The Abdication of Philosophy*, ed. Eugene Freeman (La Salle, Ill.: Open Court, 1976), pp. 157–73.

27. Berger and Kellner, *Sociology Re-Interpreted*, p. 17.

28. Berger and Luckmann, *Social Construction of Reality*, p. 20.

29. Clifford Geertz, "From the Native's Point of View," in *Symbolic Anthropology: A Reader in the Study of Symbols and Meanings*, eds. Janet Dolgin, David S. Kemnitzer, and David M. Schneider (New York: Columbia University Press, 1977); and Alfred Schutz, cited in Berger and Kellner, *Sociology Re-Interpreted*, p. 17.

30. The American people even had the opportunity to witness insurrection in the comfort of their living rooms through the medium of television. See the videotape, "The Vietnam War: An Historical Document," a narrative composed of clips from a decade of CBS news coverage.

31. Peter Berger, *Invitation to Sociology* (New York: Doubleday and Co., 1963), p. 64.

32. Durkheim's vivid analogy appears in his classic, *Suicide* (New York: The Free Press, 1951). Durkheim's approach receives thoughtful treatment in Robert Nisbet, *The Sociology of Emile Durkheim* (New York: Oxford University Press, 1974).

33. Our understanding and application of the concept of mediating structures is owed to Peter Berger and Richard J. Neuhaus, *To Empower People* (Washington, D. C.: American Enterprise Institute for Public Policy Research, 1977); and Peter Berger, "In Praise of Particularity," *Facing Up to Modernity*, pp. 130–42.

34. In the Army, a company consists of about 200 men under the command of a captain; a platoon about 40 under a lieutenant; a squad about 10 under a sergeant.

35. Cited in Berger and Neuhaus, *To Empower People*, p. 4.

36. Cited in Berger, "In Praise of Particularity," p. 132.

37. "The war of all against all" refers to "a situation in which the members of an aggregate pursue their ends by means selected only on the basis of instrumental efficiency. It presupposes that any cooperative combination is subject to immediate dissolution if, for example, exploitation or annihilation becomes more advantageous for any one member." See D. F. Aberle et al., "The Functional Prerequisites of a Society," *Ethics* 60 (January, 1950): 100–111.

38. Berger and Neuhaus use the mediating structures of family, neighborhood, church, and voluntary association to point out the ways in which human needs are met institutionally outside the megastructures. Our application of their ideas to military aggregates is justified, we believe, by the correspondence between the mediating functions they identify and the ones our Vietnam narrators reveal. The essential features of such structures are that they are "people-size" and "exist where people are."

39. Staff Sgt. Ernest Gibson of the USMC, stationed in I Corps in 1967, informed the author in conversation that there was more barbed wire strung between the Army and Marine compounds than around the perimeter to separate both from the NVA.

40. Geertz, *Interpretation of Cultures*, p. 52.

4

Walking Wounded

The more you saw, the more besides death and mutilation you risked, and the more you risked of that, the more you'd have to let go of one day as a "survivor."

—Dispatches, p. 8

The five day demonstration, organized by Vietnam Veterans Against the War, was the first time that Americans who had fought in a foreign war demanded an end to it, were not proud of being part of it, did not think it best that their country win, and hurled back the rewards they had been given for doing their duty, for being the men their fathers and the nation wanted.

—Winners and Losers, p. 329

It's taken me twelve years—it'll be thirteen in March—to assimilate the gap between what I thought I would see and what I did see.

—Everything We Had, p. 68

They gave me a Bronze Star . . . and they put me up for a Silver Star. But I said you can shove it up your ass . . . I threw all the others away. The only thing I kept was the Purple Heart because I still think I was wounded.

—Home from the War, p. 161

In the preceding chapter we traced the demise of WWII meanings and the emergence of counter-meanings through the social forms in which they were embodied. Crucial to our analysis was the recognition of the persistence of the social aspect of human existence, even under conditions that favored "the war of all against all." This analysis disclosed the pivotal function served by mediating structures in supporting the social dimension of human activity. Standing between the discredited megastructures and the precarious private sphere, the mediating formations provided an institutional "home" for the soldier whose world view had undergone cataclysmic transformation. This "home"—an interstitial zone of meaning and identity—became the central locus of social interaction through which reality was apprehended and, in turn, acted upon.

The social processes which helped to sustain this meaning and identity were touched upon only briefly. In order to understand the means by which the mediating structures enabled individuals to ward off alienation, it is necessary to examine the relationship between the individual and his institutional environment. We must extend our analysis to discern how subjective reality is socially constructed through institutionally available roles and how such role formation and role adoption organizes human activity.

In the small combat units in Vietnam, the mediating structures prescribed roles whose sole function was to ensure self-preservation. The acquisition and instantiation of this role-specific knowledge made possible a measure of symmetry between subjective and objective meanings. Due to this shaping power of the mediating structures, survival became not only a personal quest but also a collective goal toward which all social activity was geared. Furthermore, successful implementation of role-specific knowledge was a way of socially locating oneself. The individual could designate recurrent patterns of action as constitutive of a determinate "self." As Berger and Luckmann state, "In the course of action there is an identification of the self with the objective sense of the action; the action that is going on determines, for that moment, the self-apprehension of the actor, and does so in the objective sense that has been socially ascribed to the action."[1] For example, many of the soldiers' accounts include self-referential statements that are role-specific: "I was known as a definite survivor" (*N*, p. 112) or "I was a good killer, a good trooper" (*N*, p. 84). These self-definitions—linked to Vietnam War roles—have far-reaching implications for the warriors' homecoming. A good deal of attention will be devoted to this point in the following pages. The point here is the importance of the concept of role for understanding how actors define themselves and each other within any given situation.

Role theory, a particularly American contribution to social thought,[2] provides us with the necessary intellectual leverage for explaining the social dislocations experienced by the Vietnam warriors upon their return to "the World." A role, as defined earlier, is "a typified response to a typified expectation"[3] that provides the pattern according to which the individual is to act in a particular situation. The particular role will vary in the exactness with which it lays down instructions for an actor. For instance, the role of "officer" in the military is highly specific in a way that the role of "enlisted" is not. An officer's role is more narrowly prescriptive in its requirements concerning dress, language, bearing, mannerisms, and so forth than are the roles associated with lesser ranks. In fact, in most military societies an officer's significant deviation from these role demands is construed as a criminal offense. The United States Armed Forces Uniform Code of Military Justice insists upon relatively harsh punishment for an individual convicted of the charge "Conduct Unbecoming an Officer." Such a legal provision makes no sense except as a codified legitimation of the expectations adhering to the stipulated role. In contrast, it would be difficult to imagine what behavior might constitute "conduct unbecoming an enlistee." That role virtually assigns to its occupant a talent for moral delinquency. As one sociologist shrewdly observed, "In the case of elites there may even arise a code of honor which holds only for those who belong, while others are dismissed as beings somewhat less than human from whom bad manners may be expected."[4]

Moreover, roles are not simply regulatory patterns for visible behavior. As our example suggests, roles carry with them emotions and attitudes that correspond to the appropriate actions. In Peter Berger's apt phrasing, "one feels more ardent by kissing, more humble by kneeling, and more angry by shaking one's fist."[5] A role-specific performance will characteristically produce the congruent psychological reality. Roles, that is, organize and mobilize feelings which the individual perceives as suitable for the situation. Our hypothetical military officer, for instance, would experience shame and remorse for his lapse from military rectitude. He does not usually chalk up the forfeiture of his commission to the vagaries of fortune in the role-playing game. To the contrary, he obligingly assumes the role of wrongdoer without questioning the enormity of his "crime" or the appropriateness of the punishment meted out to him for it. Napoleon once remarked that he could make men willing to die for little bits of ribbon. Imagine then how the ceremonial relinquishment of those bits of ribbon affects the actors involved. As these illustrations suggest, "the sphere of psychological phenomena is continuously permeated by social forces, and more than that, is decisively shaped by the latter."[6]

Such a formulation draws our attention to a fundamental socio-psychological proposition, one that is indispensable for explaining the Vietnam veterans' world view after evacuation from the war zone: *every role has attached to it a certain identity*. Because "each role implies a world and the self is always located in a world . . . every socially constructed world thus contains a repertoire of identities and a corresponding psychological system."[7] Put simply, roles become subjectively appropriated as identities. These identities—the ways in which the individual characteristically apprehends himself, his processes of consciousness, and his relations with others—are a crucial part of the taken-for-granted assumptions about the world which every member of society "knows." For instance, "it is known as a matter 'of course' that there are men and women, that they have such-and-such psychological traits and that they will have such-and-such psychological reactions in typical circumstances."[8]

These role-governed identities vary both in duration and in degree of commitment. For purposes of illustration, consider the draftee who chooses Officers Candidate School as a means of securing optimum creature comforts in the military. He then almost certainly perceives the role of officer and its concomi-

tant identity very differently than does a recent graduate of a
service academy. For the former, the officer identity is expe-
dient and, although temporarily meaningful, trivial within the
larger framework of his biography. For the latter, however,
being an officer (and a gentleman) is fundamentally constitutive of his deepest "self." Extending the illustration beyond this
clear-cut occupational identity, consider the individual who
identifies himself as a "man." Clearly, the mere possession of
male sex organs is not sufficient to warrant such a self-defi-
nition. Indeed, as we explored in considerable detail, manhood
is a socially bestowed identity only won through demonstration of role-specific knowledge. The definitive arena for that
demonstration is, in American culture, on the field of battle.
It is there, so the successfully socialized male has been taught,
that manhood is achieved by unleashing aggression, exhibit-
ing a high tolerance to physical discomfort, and suppressing
signs of fear. Being a male is simply not equivalent to being
the socially defined and socially relative American "man."

The elements of role theory outlined above point to the fundamental insight that "identity is socially bestowed, socially
sustained, and socially transformed."[9] The process of socialization, particularly at the hands of "significant others" early
in the life cycle, provides compelling evidence for the assertion that "identity is not something 'given,' but is bestowed in
acts of social recognition."[10] Through continued social interaction with "generalized others," identity is continuously confirmed or modified according to the expectations placed upon
the actor's responses in specific social situations. In simple
terms, "men become that as which they are addressed."[11]

An instance from the Vietnam War literature will help to
clarify the socio-psychological dynamics of what Peter Berger
aptly calls "this deadly game of recognitions."[12] An American
GI who inadvertently managed to escape certain death would
immediately enjoy celebrity status by being cast in the role of
"charmed grunt." As one correspondent observed,

On operations you'd see men clustering around the charmed grunt
that many outfits created who would take himself and whoever stayed
close enough through a field of safety, at least until he rotated home

or got blown away, and then the outfit would hand the charm to someone else. If a bullet creased your head or you stepped on a dud mine or a grenade rolled between your feet and just laid there, you were magic enough. . . . I met a man in the Cav who'd been "fucking the duck" one afternoon, sound asleep in a huge tent with thirty cots inside, all empty but his, when some mortar rounds came in, tore the tent down to canvas slaw and put frags through every single cot but his, he was still high out of his mind from it, speedy, sure and lucky (D, p. 57).

What is most revealing for our purposes is the soldier's reaction to the incident in light of the expectations adhering in the "charmed grunt" role. Whereas prior to the incident that same soldier may have acted cautiously, even to the point of timidity, he would now ignore obvious risks. As predicted, the soldier's self-conception underwent drastic alteration to conform to the possibilities inherent in his new role—itself an "artifact" of the Vietnam conflict. He might, for instance, walk about above ground during an artillery barrage in an effort to demonstrate his new identity. One charmed grunt, "sitting on top of the sandbags above the trench, alone and exposed" had to be told by his sergeant "If you don't get your ass down off that berm I'll shoot you myself." Then, socially confirmed in his new identity, the GI could rejoin his comrades huddled in the relative safety of their bunker. As the reporter who witnessed this scene noted, "It made him someone special in the company. It made a lot of guys think he was lucky now, that nothing could happen to him, and they stayed as close to him as they could. I even felt some of it, enough to be glad that we were in the same bunker that night. *It made sense* [emphasis added]" (D, p. 127).

As the above illustration suggests, role theory can illuminate the social character of identity. More to the point, the integration of this theoretical contribution from social psychology with the sociology of knowledge perspective employed throughout this study enhances our understanding. Social process becomes more tractable as the concept of social role is incorporated into an overall view of the social construction of reality. The theoretical interpenetration of the two approaches can best be captured in the proposition that "identity, with its appropriate attachments of psychological reality, is always identity within a specific, socially constructed world."[13] This proposition forces our attention back to the encompassing world view in which role, identity, psychological reality—the phenomenon designated "persons"—are recognizable elements.[14]

The sociologist Erving Goffman, upon whose work we drew in our analysis of the military as a "total institution," has tested this proposition. In his research into the social universes of various kinds of inmates,[15] Goffman supplies empirical support for the assertion that "every role has a world view dangling from its end."[16] As Goffman discovered, occupants of the roles "convict" and "patient" located in the closed society of the prison or mental hospital are virtually issued, along with their institutional uniforms, a distinctive world view in and through which to make sense of their new "identity." This "social context of the self,"[17] in Goffman's terminology, enforces a highly structured and ritualized interaction that serves as the ongoing confirmation of the taken-for-granted knowledge necessary to "a society of captives."[18] The inmates, placed in a socially constructed world in which the basic assumption is that they are untrustworthy, irresponsible, and therefore in need of constant supervision, then report feelings of inferiority, weakness, and guilt. This progression simply confirms the hypothesis regarding the relationship between a socially bestowed identity and a socially constructed world.[19] In sum, "the social definition of identity takes place as part of an overarching conception of reality."[20]

Clearly, the returning warriors' experience in Vietnam had been located in a specific, socially constructed world very unlike the world they were reentering. As their own linguistic categories indicate, "the Nam" and "the World" were apprehended as disparate social universes. This distinction is one upon which a great deal hinges. Our theoretical model implies that the specific, socially constructed world of the war zone gave rise to a "Vietnam world view;" that this world view encompassed characteristically "Vietnam War roles" to which were attached "Vietnam War identities;" and that these identities embraced a distinctive "Vietnam War psychological reality." In fact, the analysis in the preceding chapter demonstrated precisely such an arrangement. A meaning system giving priority to survival made the "good killer" feel edified by his acquisition of a pair of human ears, the "fragger" take pride in his expeditious dispatch of an offending officer, the "short-timer" self-righteously refuse a lawful order, and the possessor of a "million-dollar wound" (an injury sufficiently severe to warrant permanent evacuation from the war zone but only temporarily incapacitating) experience elation, relief, and gratitude until the onset of shock rendered him semiconscious. These examples attest to the profound interpenetration of self and society posited by our social psychology/sociology of knowledge model. The complementarity of these two perspectives on social process can be summarized simply: "one identifies oneself, as one is identified by others, by being located in a common world."[21]

This proposition has enormous implications for understanding the American warriors' return to the United States. Having physically survived the "invisible enemy" in Vietnam, the soldiers returned to face a different enemy. The saga of this agonizing ordeal is still unfolding as the survivors continue to struggle for what role theory has disclosed as the *sine qua non* of meaningful identity: *social recognition*.

The postwar experience of the Vietnam veterans can best be interpreted in terms of the contradictory recognitions they were subjected to and the deprivation they underwent as a result. The Vietnam veteran, that is, was placed in a situation in which the social expectations he faced were incompatible, and therefore his sense of order was severely undermined. In social-scientific terms, the veterans endured massive and prolonged *role conflict* which led to *anomie* as the complex web of recognitions and non-recognitions the veterans encountered in "the World" rendered them "homeless." Our purpose in this chapter is to show how the society that consigned American troops to possible extinction in Southeast Asia afterwards exposed them to "chronic cognitive anxiety"[22] by thwarting their "primeval human urge to be accepted, to belong, to live in a world with others."[23] We shall attempt to understand how the veterans came to perceive themselves as deprived of the social ordering processes that confer meaning on experience and how, without such meaning, they regarded themselves as "walking wounded."

Homecoming

That's one of the most difficult re-adjustments: to re-enter the world which you were conditioned to live in since childhood, but you've gone through an experience which taught you a level of existence that you could not have imagined of yourself.

—*Nam*, p. 318

I went from a free-fire zone to the twilight zone.

—*Nam*, p. 262

Perhaps the best way to go about reconstructing the experience of the soldier who survived the war is to trace the successive steps of his separation from the military and his efforts to resume civilian life. By "freezing the action," the implications of each stage of the journey from "survivor" to "walking wounded" will emerge in detail. This strategy enables us to describe the social relations that shaped individual behavior. Moreover, it will profile the progressive attenuation of meaning and identity the soldiers underwent.

A crucial feature of the soldiers' homecoming is the disappearance of the mediating structure. This institutional arrangement—Edmund Burke's "little platoons," the source of "public affections"—had to be left behind in the initial phase of homecoming. As "buffer zones" between the "under-institutionalized" private sphere and the "over-institutionalized" public sphere they were the only collectivities capable of sustaining meaning and identity in the war zone. In a very real sense, the soldiers' estrangement from them represents a separation from "home." Power over the soldiers' fate resided, once again, solely in the hands of the bureaucratic megastructure which enforced its decisions from above without accountability to the individual.

The contrast between the two sorts of institutional forms is worth elaborating to support our thesis of role conflict resulting in anomie. One arresting aspect of the mediating structure is its responsiveness to both democratic consensus and personal initiative. Although the lineaments of military hierarchy as prescribed by Department of the Army Regulations ("the book") were observed, social life in Vietnam—including role formation and role adoption—was based almost exclusively upon the only value recognized as carrying general authority: survival. This often entailed a radical reapportionment of power in ways that directly contravened the sacred chain of command so fundamental to the administrative functioning of the megastructure.

The clearest portrayal of the mediating structure's responsiveness appears in Webb's *Fields of Fire*. When a rear-echelon colonel stupidly orders Lt. Hodges' platoon to man a vulnerable and strategically worthless listening post outside the perimeter wire, the members of the platoon balk. After a debate over the best way to get the order countermanded, the outfit arrives at a consensus. They present their case to Hodges for consideration by the colonel's staff. Hodges listens carefully to his troops' arguments, concurs with the outfit's reasoning, and endeavors to have the order rescinded by command center. What transpires at command center is especially revealing for the mediating/megastructure contrast pursued here:

Hodges approached a jowly, stocky First Lieutenant, who apparently was running the command center, and attempted to explain Snake's reasoning. The First Lieutenant glowered impatiently as Hodges spoke . . . finally . . . cutting Hodges off.

"How long you been in Vietnam, Lieutenant?" He emphasized the "Lieutenant" in an apparent attempt to distinguish his seniority.

Hodges shrugged unconcernedly. "A month or so."

The First Lieutenant scowled impatiently. "Well, look. We've got more than four years of Vietnam inside this bunker, just among the officers. We know what we're doing. Don't tell us how to do our job."

"Look yourself. I don't care if you've been here all your goddamn life." Hodges smiled calmly. "No disrespect to the Colonel intended, you understand. But that don't mean you can't take a suggestion. I

think my man has a good point. LPs on the other side of this wire
are crazy as hell" (*FF*, p. 127).

Of course, Hodges' claim is rejected, and a squad is sent out
to the LP where they later suffer heavy casualties from at-
tacking enemy soldiers and from the American artillery barrage called in to repel these attackers. The scene's relevance
for us, however, lies not in the ultimate deployment of Third
Platoon's combat troops but in the depiction of the two lieu-
tenants' conflicting concerns. By questioning rather than blindly
obeying the wisdom of command center, Hodges acts contrary
to the expectations constitutive of the role of officer. Instead
of identifying with the roles the megastructure provides, Hodges
legitimates the moral authority of the social formation "below" and the course of action it has pragmatically chosen. Using Hodges as a symbol of mediating structures' responsiveness, we witness a power arrangement approximating the
democratic ideal. The perennially scowling First Lieutenant
clearly represents opposite tendencies. Rigid and unyielding,
he personifies the megastructure's reliance upon coercion as
the foundation of authority. He ruthlessly enforces the impersonal decision-making prerogatives of the chain of command.
The mediating structures are simply institutionally more open
to "grass-roots initiatives."

To heighten further the contrast between the two social formations, especially as they mandate roles and identities, mediating structures engage in "person selection"[24] on a more
intimate basis than do the large institutions. Person selection,
according to Hans Gerth and C. Wright Mills, refers to the
process by which every social structure chooses those individuals it needs for its functioning. The goal towards which that
functioning is geared will, of course, vary from society to society. In a culture in which imperial conquest is acknowledged
as the *summum bonum* of earthly existence, fierce warriors will
be selected for canonization and pacifists for anathemazation.
"The grandeur that was Rome," for example, was made possible by such a process of person selection as was its downfall
at the hands of the barbarians.[25]

The goal of group survival in Vietnam involved the mediating structure in just such a process of person selection. Cer-

tain GIs with traits defined as socially desirable, i.e., which enhanced the platoon's chances for survival, enjoyed high status and exercised considerable power regardless of their military rank. As one reporter noted, "If you had any extra-sense capacity, if you could smell VC or their danger the way hunting guides smelled the coming weather, if you had special night vision, or great ears, you were magic" (*D*, p. 57). Conversely, if a soldier exhibited traits that rendered him a social liability, he would suffer social ostracism. Ironically, the least desirable identity one could assume was that of "hero." The "hero" and his equivalent, the "cowboy," were detested because their actions could result in unnecessary casualties. For instance, a seasoned veteran might inform a comrade temporarily occupying the role of FNG (Fucking New Guy) not to "go trying to be a hero, because all you're going to do is get killed" (*EWH*, p. 159). In the last years of the war, the much-publicized Green Berets were shunned because "they got all kinds of cowboys in there, and the cowboys wanted to go out and shoot and kick down doors and beat up people. The Special Forces become overpopulated with cowboys. And I think that's the demise of Special Forces" (*EWH*, p. 201).

Two examples from *Fields of Fire* further illustrate how person selection in the mediating structure modified, and even directly violated, the role assignments and the repertoire of identities in the megastructure. In Hodges' platoon, power belongs to those possessing specialized bodies of knowledge essential for the group's continued survival. The soldier nicknamed Snake, for instance, made all decisions in actual or potential combat situations. His familiarity with the habits of the invisible enemy and his coolness under fire earned him the role of platoon tactician, despite his relatively low rank of corporal. He is empowered to bark orders that are to be obeyed even by those whom he must, in other situations, address as "Sir." Similarly, the private called Catman is the unquestioned policymaker while the platoon is patrolling. Endowed with especially acute vision and an almost preternatural "feel" for terrain, Catman plays the role of scout, the eyes and ears of the platoon. A clump of earth in an otherwise unremarkable field signals to him the presence of land mines, or shallow

graves, or perhaps an enemy tunnel complex. While travers-
ing terrain, Catman runs Third Platoon. These examples point
out the unique role-playing and identity-building processes
particular to mediating structures as "people-size" social institutions.

Contrast this process of identity bestowal with that of "the
disidentifying world of the megastructure."[26] Person selection
there depended, at least in part, on "willingness to accept pettiness, untruths, a rigid and relentless pecking order" (*WL*,
p. 251). Officers were selected by the military society almost
solely on the basis of loyalty and length of service to that society—neither of which automatically confers leadership skills.
Unlike the platoon, the U. S. Army's size made it impractica-
ble to engage in person selection on the basis of intimate ac-
quaintance. Rather, the megastructure stuck rigidly to the
policy of vertical recruitment institutionally reified in the abstract chain of command. Having made such an administrative commitment, the institution then had to inculcate the belief "that mere rank made a person more intelligent,
compensated for personal deficiencies" (*FF*, p. 129). As one
commentator shrewdly observed, "Despite all the double-talk
in this area that is customary in so-called democratic armies,
such as the American one, one of the fundamental implications is that an officer is a superior somebody, entitled to obe-
dience and respect on the basis of this superiority."[27] The
Vietnam warriors' violent de-objectivation of this component
of the military belief-system, "fragging," was total.

This relatively impersonal person selection indicates that in
certain social contexts identity is socially enjoined rather than
socially bestowed. Person selection accomplished on the basis
of only a superficial knowledge of individuals frequently results in a less than ideal correspondence between institutional requirements and individual aptitude. Nonetheless, the
large social agglomerates of the public sphere have at their
disposal the requisite mechanisms of social control, including
a virtual monopoly of the instruments of violence, to ensure
compliance. Person selection in the megastructure is thus accomplished on the basis of what we might call a ruthless instrumental inefficiency. In the Armed Forces, for example, the

raw material (the trainee) is processed to fill a particular need for which that material may be spectacularly unsuited. Of course, even the U. S. Army will not draft a blind man and send him to war. But, as the Vietnam War narratives demonstrate, it will select fools for officers, scoundrels for NCOs, and psychopaths for soldiers.

The soldier named Goodrich in *Fields of Fire*, for example, enlisted in the U. S. Marine Corps to play in the Marine Marching Band. Promised a slot in this august body by his recruiter, the talented ex-Harvard musician winds up where the Corps needs him: in a line company in Vietnam. There he loses a limb and gets several of his countrymen killed through his ineptness as a combat rifleman. A similar point is made in the nonfiction tour-de-force *M* in which the method whereby American GIs are selected for combat duty in Vietnam is depicted. The obvious symbol for the callous assignment of duty (and identity) is the Pentagon. There a Major Pulver reduces the complexities of human character to the stereotypical number on a computer card. Not so incidentally, the computer operator has himself experienced such arbitrary person selection in the megastructure. His physical description as a mild-mannered, pipe-smoking, doting parent belies the identity-that-might-have-been. Early in his military career, Pulver had "asked for infantry first, tanks second, artillery third, he was granted none of these, and, as a young second-lieutenant of engineers he asked for Korea but he was flown to Germany" (*M*, p. 22). Clearly, an equally capricious fate awaits the soldiers whose destination (and destiny) Pulver's computer cards will determine:

Every man in the Army after he was through training would be assigned a duty station by Major Pulver. This winter morning he had a stack of those stiff IBM cards the size of an old British pound note, one apiece for every soldier in M. These cards had green edges, and Pulver had a second deck of colorless IBM cards, one apiece for everywhere on Earth that the Army had an opening. . . . Were the IBM cards to be believed, none of M's two hundred and fifty soldiers wanted to go to Vietnam. . . . Doing it the Army way he would need to take any green card and white card and fasten them together with a paper clip (*M*, p. 22).

Clearly, person selection and therefore identity allocation in the administratively complex megastructure is not amenable to "grass-roots initiative." In sum, the megastructures are "remote, hard to understand, or downright unreal, impersonal and ipso facto unsatisfactory for the discovery and actualization of individual meaning and identity. In the classical Marxian term, the megastructures are 'alienating.' "[28] It is to these megastructures that the soldiers were now entrusted for homecoming.

The two types of social organization within the military and the social relations that characterize each illustrate the role-sponsoring and identity-generating function of institutions. The discrepancy between the roles sponsored by the mediating structure and those available in and through the larger social formations has implications that are far from trivial.

Most importantly, the GI remanded to the custody of the megastructure for reentry into civilian life experienced profound social dislocation. Drawing upon our socio-psychological model, we can account for this distress with a seeming paradox: homecoming caused homesickness. More precisely, the troops experienced role conflict as a result of the asymmetry between their socially bestowed identity and the socially constructed world to which that identity was suddenly whisked. As one soldier described the process of homecoming: "I left Vietnam and thirty-seven and a half hours later I was home. Home in the middle of fucking November, drizzle and 32 degrees. No transition. Fucking weird" (N, p. 284). Structurally, the usually symbiotic relationship between identity and the world had collapsed. Put differently, the "fit" between self and world was strained to the breaking point by the unusual circumstances of the Vietnam warriors' homecoming.[29] As one soldier tells of his sudden, almost magical passage from the Nam to the World: "I still don't know exactly what that did to me. It is something that I haven't gotten over and don't expect to, somehow" (N, p. 241). In sum, the reciprocal nature of organism and environment was shattered.

An elaboration of the way this reciprocity functioned successfully in Vietnam may clarify the point. A soldier, for example, identifying himself, as he was identified by others, as

"Corporal-By-Dint-of-Two-Combat-Meritorious-Promotions-and Life-Saving-Strategist-of-Lt.-Hodges'-Platoon-in-Company-B" inhabited a secure identity protected from anomic disintegration. That is, he occupied an "address" which supplied the coordinates of the self. Furthermore, this series of recognitions enabled the GI to appropriate not only an identity but also a world: a class world of "Corporals," a moral world of "Life-Savers," a kinship world of "Platoons," an achievement world of "Meritorious Promotions," and so forth. Reality was cognitively meaningful because the individual had an unambiguous place of residence within it. As this extrapolated description of Corporal Snake from *Fields of Fire* suggests, it is the fit between socially bestowed identity and socially constructed world that renders him "a comprehending denizen, master of a violent world" (*FF*, p. 332).

The megastructure required that an identity such as his— painstakingly constructed through a socio-psychological process akin to triangulation—be relinquished as an initial condition of homecoming. The GI, in fact, was stripped of an identity bestowed by a series of social recognitions of often bewildering complexity to a simple, "disidentifying" one: "returnee." In the words of one ex-warrior, "Returnees is an Army word, a word no one else would use" (*IID*, p. 204). The GI-qua-returnee was immediately placed in an alien social surround, usually a base camp populated by other anonymous returnees. One soldier responded to the institutional reality of his new home by saying, "In the rear area, protected from the war by rows of bunkers and rolls of barbed wire, I joined the real United States Army" (*IID*, p. 177).

This phase is the initial part of a process clarified in our analysis of basic training in the military. Just as the civilian there was kept isolated from normal role referents, the combatant about to become a civilian had to be similarly manipulated. This procedure helps to avert the predictable consequences of inappropriate role performances. A Navy scout recalls,

All you were supposed to do over there was be crazy, so we were crazy. It wasn't something that we turned on and off. . . . I was insane the

entire time I was in Vietnam. In fact, even when we got back to the
United States they were going to lock us up. They said, "We don't
know what to do with you guys. You're taking on the Imperial Beach
Police Department. You're beating up Hell's Angels. You're doing all
this crazy stuff, jumping off piers and insane things" (*EWH*, p. 212).

This sailor's behavior illustrates the necessity of ensuring a
deep initial break with past roles, what Goffman calls "role
dispossession."[30]
   One of the roles which every GI briefly occupied in the mediating structure before role assignment as a returnee was
"short-timer." The prestigious identity attached to this role
conferred elevated social status and exempted its bearer from
performing especially dangerous duties. One journalist perceptively analyzes what he calls the "Short-Timer Syndrome"
precisely in terms of role expectations: "no one expects much
from a man when he is down to one or two weeks. He becomes
a luck freak, an evil-omen collector, a diviner of every bad sign"
(*D*, p. 91). A soldier who thus identified himself, as he was
identified by others, as a "short-timer" could speak with authority on Vietnam because of his impressive credentials: a body
which had survived a tour of duty. In contrast, the identity of
"returnee" was subject to a leveling process that rendered every
soldier, at least in the eyes of the megastructure under whose
jurisdiction he now fell, simply another anonymous GI, albeit
breathing, to be shipped like cargo stateside.
   An appreciation of the particular roles at stake in this instance of role dispossession and role reassignment explains why
a number of the troops, including those openly opposed to the
war, volunteered to serve another tour of duty. The GI who,
in military parlance, "extended" thereby escaped role dispossession and reaped the psychological benefits of retaining social standing. As Goffman forcefully reminds us, "Although
some roles can be re-established . . . it is plain that other losses
are irrevocable and painfully experienced as such."[31]
   A soldier who extended didn't undergo transformation from
a socially envied "short-timer" to an indistinguishable and un-
distinguished "returnee," but to someone altogether unusual:
a character "on his second tour." Although an individual "on

his second tour" had to expose himself to the dangers from which, by social convention, the "short-timer" was excused, his new identity carried other compensations. For instance, a "second tour" GI was granted nearly total immunity from the regulations concerning dress, protocol, personal habits, and even criminal conduct which the megastructure imposed upon lesser citizens. One reporter tells of a "third tour Lurp" (Long Range Recon Patroller) sporting "a gold earring and headband torn from a piece of camouflage parachute material, and since nobody was about to tell him to get his hair cut it fell below his shoulders covering a thick purple scar" (D, p. 6). Such privileges were only accorded those with special status. This status was measured by the same standard as the "short-timer's": time incountry. In addition, a multiple-tour GI received a promotion and a chance to join one of the elite units. Having demonstrated the requisite commitment and motivation upon which those groups prided themselves, a common "ground-pounder" or "grunt" on his first tour could wind up a Lurp, Recondo, SEAL, or Air Commando on his second. In the enforced conformity of military society, the special insignia and special gear these crack troops display are symbols of distinction not to be scoffed at. In a cruel irony common to social life generally, preserving status meant adopting an identity that might prove self-destructive.

Goffman's work with inmate societies is a reminder that any socially supported identity protects the individual from the chaos threatening to engulf him. "On the level of meaning, the institutional order represents a shield against terror. To be anomic, therefore, means to be deprived of this shield and to be exposed, alone, to the onslaught of nightmare."[32] Role dispossession intentionally strips one of a particular institutional order in which one's identity is established. In this way, the transformation from "short-timer" within the mediating structure posed a genuine menace to meaning.

Moreover, because identity is subject to habitualization, the individual in a total institution like the military is subject to "disculturation." This "untraining" renders him unable to manage features of daily life outside the institution.[33] Although disculturation is most commonly observed in older inmates confined for long periods of time, the soldiers' accounts reveal that the process can depend on the intensity of experience inside the institution, irrespective of duration. A tour of duty in Vietnam demanded such a thorough reorientation to reality that the result was disculturation. Like its classic victims, the veterans report "growing old" in the war zone: "In the span of months, [we] passed from boyhood through manhood to a premature middle age. . . . We left Vietnam peculiar creatures, with young shoulders that bore rather old heads" (*RW*, p. xv); "I saw that face at least a thousand times at a hundred bases and camps, all the youth sucked out of the eyes, the color drawn from the skin, cold white lips. . . . Life had made him old. He'd live it out old. All those faces, serious beyond what you'd call their years if you didn't know for yourself what the minutes and hours of those years were made up of" (*D*, p. 16).

Both role dispossession and disculturation are causes of that most dreaded of all social diseases: anomie. In combination they posed a formidable threat to meaning and identity that compelled many soldiers to "extend." The narratives offer a wealth of testimony that the GIs needed to feel "at home" in a social world. Intuitively aware of the disjunction between the identity-generating features of the social institutions we have analyzed, one soldier remarked, "It was kind of nice over there in a way. *Even the Army couldn't get to you.* What are they going to do, send you to Nam? I hadn't been home for fifteen months. *I was more afraid of going home than of staying there* [emphasis added]" (*N*, p. 280). Another recalls, "I was going to stay a third year but they gave me a year early out and made me go back home. Some guys they had to lock up because they wouldn't leave Vietnam" (*N*, p. 266). A third, acutely aware of status considerations, said, "In Nam they called grunts kings. I walked with kings. These people were going to get shit on when they came back here, but in Vietnam they were kings" (*N*, p. 264). Perhaps Corporal Snake's observations exemplify the beliefs of all "extenders": "If he were to go back now—when he did go back—there was nothing, not a thing, that would parallel the sense of urgency and authority and—need. Of being a part of something. And of being needed and being good. . . .

The heart-rending deaths. The successes. All here. None there, back in the bowels of the World. . . . Extend? Hell, yeah. I'll extend until this goddamn thing is over" (*FF*, p. 333). It is the social recognition—the identity—of "being needed and being good" that explain Snake's behavior and also, as we shall see, the behavior of those who did not "extend."

The related mystery of soldiers reenlisting ("re-upping") after receiving their discharge papers in order to return to Vietnam can also be explained in this way. Perhaps the only difference between the two groups of "Nam addicts" is that those who attempted civilian life had even more reason to return to the war. Dramatizing the rigors of role dispossession and disculturation, one soldier recounts, "I signed in wearing my civilian clothes. I'm all alone and feeling discombobulated. It was just too much, too quick for me. I said to myself, 'No man. I don't want no part of this.' There was only one thing on my mind: *Get back to Vietnam where I felt at home. I felt so much like I didn't belong in America.* What are you going to do? How are you going to talk to somebody? I went back there to get it over quick, but it never came [emphasis added]" (*N*, p. 266). "Before I got there I was scared and I was thinking I shouldn't go into that world. Once I got in Nam, there was no turning back. Your mind clicks and it's hard for it to click back. I couldn't adjust back now unless they created a Nam, the same thing with the incoming and the shooting. Then I'd be happy as a punk in Boy's Town. I could survive" (*N*, p. 306). One correspondent recounts that a Lurp confided, "I just can't hack it back in the World." This same soldier related "that after he'd come back home the last time he would sit in his room all day, and sometimes he'd stick a hunting rifle out the window, leading people and cars as they passed his house until the only feeling he was aware of was all up in the tip of one finger. 'It used to put my folks real uptight,' he said" (*D*, p. 5). Still others say simply, "As bad as it was in Nam, I knew exactly what to expect there" (*N*, p. 280); and "*I just wanted to get back to Vietnam where I belong. I really felt I belonged there* [emphasis added]" (*N*, p. 266). As our extended and re-upped informants affirm, exposure to physical peril was preferable to the onslaught of anomie.

In the next section we shall examine the reactions the veterans met with in the United States. These reactions convinced even those who never considered extending that if "home" was certainly not among the corpses and minefields of Indochina, neither was it where they had left it thirteen months earlier. We shall, that is, attempt to understand the way the identity of "returnee" was supplanted through acts of social recognition with that of "outcast"—how Vietnam's defenders became "America's pariahs."

America's Pariahs

> I thought I would come home as a war hero, you know. I didn't really want to be a war hero, but I thought I'd get a lot of respect because I'd done something for my country. Somewhere in my psyche I thought that people would react to what I'd done and say, "Hey, great job. Good work."
> —*Nam*, p. 269

> Nobody wants to listen. . . . We are like voices from the Tomb. We remind them of death too much. They don't want to listen.
> —*Winners and Losers*, p. 33

Although the "returnee's" actual departure from South Vietnam was a critical step in the homecoming ritual, rarely was it an occasion for celebration. From the moment the returnee boarded the plane bound for "the World," he was thrust into a universe of alien meanings. As one soldier reports while still on Vietnamese soil, "The airplane smells and feels artificial. The stewardess, her carefree smile and boredom flickering like bad lighting, doesn't understand. It's enraging because you sense she doesn't want to understand. There is no joy in leaving. Nothing to savor with your eyes or heart" (*IID*, p. 202). This GI's perception of the World's incomprehension and indifference is prophetic, although the full extent of that unconcern will not show itself until his airplane reaches its ultimate destination: "the land of the Big PX" (*D*, p. 2).

We have already discussed the implications of a socio-psychological model of identity, especially the ways in which identity is socially bestowed in and through roles, the institutions that provide forms for them, and the overarching conception of reality they presuppose. It is now necessary to extend our investigation to include the processes whereby identity is *socially transformed* as well.

As "the Nam addicts" (the extenders and re-uppers) demonstrated, it is possible for "an individual to become so habituated to certain identities that, even when his social situation changes, he has difficulty keeping up with the expectations newly directed at him."[34] "The Nam addicts" became "stuck" in the social universe of the mediating structure by locking into the roles available within it. Those roles—"Lurps, SEALs, recondos, Green Beret Bushmasters, redundant mutilators, heavy rapers, eye-shooters, widow-makers, nametakers, pointmen, isolatos, and outriders, classic essential American types" (*D*, p. 34)—functioned within their institutional context to confer identity upon actors and thus provide meaning for their everyday experience. The difficulty these combat troops encountered was precisely in meeting the expectations the megastructure directed at them in preparation for civilian life. They were, in fact, simply incapable of obligingly assuming the identity of returnee on the way to full non-military status. In their own tragic way, "the Nam addicts" provide evidence for the sociological proposition that "the transformability of the self depends not only on its social context, but also on the degree of habituation to previous identities."[35]

Habituation obviously depends upon a number of variables, including the desirability of a particular identity within its milieu. In the war zone, practical utility was one variable that exerted tremendous influence. On a scale of instrumental usefulness, the physical continuity of the organism—sheer survival—was bound to rank at the very top. The soldiers became habituated to their Vietnam War identities because their very existence demanded mastery of the role-specific knowledge constitutive of those identities. It follows that the soldiers could not automatically surrender those combat-honed identities upon landing on American soil.

Rather, they underwent identity transformation through precisely the same process as their previous metamorphosis into warriors: internalization of the complex web of recognitions and non-recognitions in which they were suspended. It is these recognitions, and especially their incommensurability, that warrant investigation. Such an investigation will show how a particular self-image comes to be repudiated and an alternative one defined and assimilated—in this case the change from "returnee" to "pariah."

An understanding of identity transformation, what Berger calls "alternation,"[36] involves scrutinizing the social processes through which it is achieved. Not only the content of the recognitions that structure an individual's identity requires specification but also the social location of those actors sponsoring the recognitions. That is, we need to take such recognitions out of the ether called "society" and pinpoint them in the particular social milieux in which they actually operate. Although the Vietnam War narratives provide only anecdotal evidence for making such a determination, some useful distinctions can be addressed. The best way to take up these distinctions is in light of reference group theory.

The concept of reference groups has become one of the central analytic tools within social psychology for explaining a wide range of phenomena.[37] Most generally, the term designates "some identifiable grouping to which an actor is related in some manner and the norms and values shared in that group."[38] For the purpose of analyzing "alternation," the concept's range of meaning can be narrowed to include only "that group whose perspective constitutes the frame of reference of the actor."[39] In more familiar terms, a reference group is that collectivity which determines an individual's world view and, ipso facto, his identity in that social world. Reference group theory cautions us to bear in mind that people live in particular and discrete bounded social universes of other actual persons rather than in "a culture" per se. Moreover, each of these worlds extracts specific cognitive commitments. One concise formulation of this concept is "every group to which one refers oneself occupies a vantage point on the universe."[40]

Furthermore, a reference group is not necessarily a collectivity to which an individual belongs or even aspires to belong. For instance, a member of a minority group may hate the dominant majority yet still see the world largely through its eyes. A reference group may be envied or despised or even imaginary,[41] provided its perspective is the one assumed by the actor. That is, reference groups, regardless of how they are evaluated, "arise through the internalization of norms; they constitute the structure of expectations imputed to some audience for whom one organizes his conduct."[42]

It is through reference groups, "cliques of world-builders hammering out their models of the cosmos,"[43] that identity is socially bestowed. One does not, that is, come by one's self-apprehension by appeal to the "Zeitgeist" or "society" *tout court* but through acknowledgment of "the confirming responses of other people."[44] Reference group theory obliges us to scrutinize not only the contents of those responses but also the influence of the agents sponsoring them. Reference group theory mandates the "irritating interjection of the question 'Says who?' into the grand debate of Weltenschauungen."[45] Most significantly for our purposes, "much of the interest in reference groups arises out of concerns with situations in which a person is confronted with the necessity of choosing between two or more organized perspectives."[46]

The Vietnam vet was placed in such a situation from the moment he neared completion of his tour of duty. Summarily deprived of his reference group, his platoon, upon becoming a "returnee," the soldier faced role conflict. After separation from the military, the veteran again found himself confronted by two dramatically divergent interpretations of reality, each prescribing roles to which were attached identities. Both interpretations, upon internalization, made conflict a dominant feature of the veteran's biography. By a now-familiar process, these interpretations became objectivated and maintained through ongoing social interaction. Interpretations imposed upon the ex-warriors by their reference groups became true descriptions as a consequence of the human activity in which they were embedded. These "interpretations" or "confirming responses" or "recognitions" taught the soldiers to understand themselves not as survivors of a senseless tragedy but as

"America's pariahs"—social outcasts to be ignored or reviled. The world's initial response serving to confirm this identity was a deafening silence—the absence of recognitions with which the warriors were met. As one soldier describes it, "I was going to rent a car and drive home. I thought of visiting my parents. And I thought, 'This is the last time I'm going to have to do this again.' How anticlimactic it was. Nobody met me at the airport. Nobody knew I was coming home" (*EWH*, p. 78). Such bathos was typical. The Vietnam warriors, returning one by one or in shifts over the span of almost a dozen years, drew no dramatic public acclaim to mark the end of sacrifice for God and country. The most wrenching experience of their young lives went unremarked, a rite-of-passage aborted. Their "debut" as combat veterans was ruined by a non-recognition that informed them: "It never happened. You are invisible."

This message proved especially confusing for these Americans, nurtured on their father's tales of VE and VJ days. The American myth of the returning conqueror included celebration and raucous spectacles signifying the community's gratitude: cheering, shouting, back-slapping, drink-buying, kissing, hugging, waving—the culture's "embrace." Moreover, that embrace traditionally incorporated highly structured and even somber ceremonies to commemorate the soldiers' noble sacrifice: parades, speeches, bunting and banners, testimonials, public prayer, awards. Except for the POWs, most Vietnam-era troops were met with "a permanent sign in the Mess Hall, 'Welcome Home, Returnees.'" (*IID*, p. 204). Such conspicuous apathy, tantamount to dismissal, posed particularly acute problems of interpretation for the veteran struggling to fashion an identity that accorded with his new civilian status.

This indifference had a devastating impact. Perhaps the anomie-generating capacity of such non-recognitions is greater than that of specific recognitions, no matter how odious. The force of non-recognition admits of no debate. There is simply no adequate response to the threat non-recognition poses to identity. One soldier declaimed, "There were a lot of people that I knew still over in Vietnam, while all these other people were doing their fucking Christmas shopping as if nothing else was happening in the world. That's trite, but that's the way I felt.

I wanted somebody to pick a fight with me. I was ready to hit anybody who got in my way over anything" (*N*, p. 285). This desire for confrontation (counter-definition) went unfulfilled. Echoes of this disappointment reverberate throughout the troops' accounts. As one battle-scarred veteran told his commanding officer after returning to Vietnam, "Airplane drivers still drive their airplanes. Businessmen still run their businesses. College kids still go to college. It's like nothing really happened, except to other people. It isn't *touching* anybody except us. It makes me sick, Lieutenant" (*FF*, p. 210).

The soldiers were caught in a particularly vicious bind. Those completing their tour during the early phases of the war were met with a genuine ignorance of U. S. military commitments while those serving after the American public became disgusted with the war were shunned as "losers." One of the former recalls, "Almost no one in the Washington area knew we had anything like what was going on in Vietnam. Those of us who had been there wore our military patches on our right shoulders, which denoted that we had been in the war. Colonels would stop me and say, 'What war you been in, son? We have people fighting over there?'" (*EWH*, p. 11). One of the latter observes that "If it had happened in WWII they still would be telling stories about it. They don't even tell recruits about it today. Marines don't talk about Vietnam. We lost. They never talk about losing. So it's just wiped out, all of that's off the slate, it doesn't count. It makes you a little bitter" (*EWH*, p. 29). Another soldier tells of his discovery upon returning to the United States, "I was shocked because I didn't know we lost the war. We weren't losing while I was there" and sums up the issue of non-recognition succinctly by saying, "Coming back to America, I was shocked, not by the fact that no one cared, but that no one even talked about it" (*N*, p. 314).

This haunting silence is crucial for understanding one facet of the soldiers' role conflict. Traditionally, the returning veteran role obligates one to recount events which transpired on the fields of fire. Like their fathers, upon whose accounts their young imaginations fed, the Vietnam veterans were bursting with stories of courage, fear, compassion, sacrifice, and camaraderie. These components are basic to war, even an otherwise tainted one. They constitute the raw materials out of which culturally mediated conceptions of human possibility are forged. In fact, the psycho-historian Robert J. Lifton has argued that it is the solemn duty of warriors in every culture to bear witness. Lifton claims that all societies pay homage to "the life-trajectory of the warrior: the call to adventure, the crossing of the threshold into another realm of action and experience, the road of trials, and eventually the return to his people to whom he can convey a new dimension of wisdom."[47] Such a crucial function, Lifton asserts, enables the warrior to "connect with, and reinforce, the immortalizing currents of his society and culture."[48] Whether or not we concur with the pancultural and trans-historical sweep of Lifton's proposition, clearly, American soldiers returned expecting to speak their urgent truths. Quite incomprehensibly, they, unlike their forbears, were sentenced to silence.

This conspicuous absence of "conversation" had enormous consequences. Most significantly, the silence with which the soldiers were greeted resulted, very quickly, in a self-imposed "gag order." As one GI tells, "I casually mentioned the bottle of Vick's we used to kill the stench of the dead on the airplanes by rubbing it in our nostrils. . . . You can chase people through all the words of all the languages, as Yossarian attempted, but you'll never make them understand. Never. So you give up trying" (WL, p. 6). As our socio-psychological model predicts, the non-recognition conveyed its message directly into the subjective consciousness of the vets. In theoretical terminology, "the psychological reality of the socialized individual thus verifies subjectively what his society has objectively defined as real."[49] The veteran, like certain kinds of handicapped or deformed individuals in American culture, went overlooked and unheard. By assimilating and internalizing the message communicated in the eyes-averted and ears-plugged stance of the "silent majority" of his countrymen, the ex-GI appropriated a new identity: pariah. Precisely because identity is social in character, one returnee reported, "I went back to school that September. I paid my own way to school. I didn't want to get my GI benefits because I didn't want nobody to know I was a veteran. I was ashamed because everybody in the U. S. hated GIs for being in the Nam. I was trying to hide myself" (*N*, p. 289). A similar note is struck by the soldier incorporating the expectation that Vietnam vets should be neither seen nor heard: "Before I went over, I knew a couple of friends who came back. And when I came back I ended up the same way. Almost mute" (*EWH*, p. 132).

Reference group theory insists we ask, Who was this "silencing majority" bestowing the pariah identity through acts of non-recognition? The answer is simple. By and large, those we have identified as "significant others" extracted a vow of silence. It was not a world of faceless strangers that turned a deaf ear to the soldiers but their own Gemeinschaft world of parents, friends, and neighbors. These consociates, with whom social interaction has the most telling consequences, were responsible for neglecting the vets and thereby making this alternation possible.

This reference group's behavior is explicable only by recalling that the Vietnam War inflicted none of the domestic hardship and social dislocation that characterized the Paradigm War, World War II. Unlike the darker days of the fight against Fascism, the war against godless Communism required no material sacrifices from the folks on the home front: no "meatless Wednesdays," no rationing coupons, no shortages, no autos garaged "for the duration" so that precious gasoline and rubber could be allocated to the "war effort." Even the traditional hallmark of America-at-war, Liberty Bonds, was nowhere to be found. Just the reverse held true. The Vietnam War fueled a surge in economic growth and material well-being across the entire class spectrum of American society. From the most highly skilled technician to the lowliest manual laborer, the Vietnam War proved an economic blessing.[50] Hence, with the possible exception of fatter paychecks and lower unemployment rates, civilian life in America proceeded apace. The principal tasks of the American citizenry—earning a living, raising a family, and worshipping a benign and not-too-judgmental God—continued uninterrupted by the slaughter taking place in an obscure country half a world away. Against this backdrop, the truths vouchsafed the veterans by their war experience looked especially threatening. As one bitter re-upper put it, "We been abandoned, Lieutenant. We been kicked off the edge of the goddamned cliff. They don't know how to fight it, and they don't know how to stop fighting it. And back home it's too complicated, so they forget about and do their rooting at football games. Well, fuck 'em. They ain't worth dying for" (*FF*, p. 210). After listening to a Viet vet harangue him about the inhumanity being committed in his name, one "abandoner" bluntly confessed, "What you say seems to be true. But I just don't care. I am a white, red-headed Irishman, and I care most about other white, red-headed Irishmen like myself. I can't worry too much about blacks or gooks" (*HFW*, p. 146). For the Vietnam veteran, "out of sight, out of mind" wasn't just a tired cliché; it was the imposition of a cruel and unusual punishment.

The family, a reference group traditionally responsible for identity maintenance and even identity repair, inflicted a terrible blow to the sons' self-regard. The soldiers served their sentences of silence most painfully around the dining room table. Indoctrinated into "war consciousness" by fathers proud of their exploits in the Second World War, the soldiers returned to find "the old man" much less attentive than anticipated. The soldiers insist that the fathers' unwillingness to face the enormity of Vietnam stemmed from their own cognitive commitments as fiercely patriotic veterans of a foreign war. In the words of one father whose sentiments are typical, "I wouldn't be destroyed because I've been in war, I know that in war there's death. So the kid has a bit of a hard time living in the outdoors, but it'll make a man out of him. It's what you make of it . . . if you want to look at the bad side of things, then Vietnam could be rough. There'll always be war" (*WL*, p. 262). Even when the fatherly response was not quite so callous, the fathers avoided upsetting their own cognitive applecarts. In an exchange of dialogue across cognitive universes as well as generations, this dilemma is dramatized:

"Well, I'm glad it's over for you, Son. It must have been terrible."
    "It'll never be over, Dad. Most of it hasn't even happened yet" (*FF*, p. 392).

The father's interpretation of Vietnam—a traumatic experience best handled by allowing memory to erase its traces—

conflicts with the son's mounting conviction that horror on that scale is not so easily expunged. As another veteran observes, "The war's not over for us. It won't be over until somebody takes their rightful responsibility" (*N*, p. 311).

As the other accounts of family reunions indicate, this snatch of conversation is paradigmatic. Other members of the nuclear family betray a similar uneasiness with the stranger in their midst. Traditionally protected by their role from hearing the clinical details of bloodshed, mothers also had difficulty relating to the moody character posing as the son of a year earlier. This boy, having in twelve months grown into middle-aged cynicism, provoked confusion and hurt. As one vet remembers, "My mother told my brother, 'Leave Steve alone, he's not the same anymore.'" (*EWH*, p. 255). Even siblings suffered estrangement from one another during a twelve-month separation that might as accurately have been measured in light years: "Later, when we got home, my brother said, 'Don't wear your uniform.' What kind of shit was that? I wanted to wear the fucking thing. I had my ribbons. I'm a king. That didn't hurt me then, but it hurts me now" (*N*, p. 274). The family, violating its traditional function as refuge from non-recognition and anomie, contributed instead to it. In so doing, it aided and abetted the soldiers' self-identification as "America's pariahs."

Equally damning was the silence of those who had figured prominently in the soldiers' pre-Vietnam War experience. Friends and neighbors, the actors who constitute any Gemeinschaft, preferred to ignore the veteran because of the urgent issues which he, sometimes merely by his presence, raised. As one returnee recounts, "I dropped back into the old neighborhood and nothing had changed. They were the same people in the same situation with the same head. There's been no time passing for them. It was like I never left. Well, I *did* leave. I wasn't the same anymore" (*N*, p. 264). Another insists that "There's still alot of things that I'm real close to in there. But the people I know say, 'Forget it. It's over.' People want me to bury it. I can't bury it. I did learn something and I'm not sure what. But I know it affected me a whole lot" (*EWH*, p. 255–56). Thus, the "community," as that term designates a particular reference group of significant others, condemned the soldiers to social invisibility and confirmed them in their "walking wounded" role.

If this non-recognition devalued the Vietnam War identities to which the vets were habituated, the recognition they did receive positively assaulted that identity. That recognition, the "GI as war criminal," proclaimed them as being truly beyond the pale: death-tainted marauders forfeiting all claims to a common humanity. Communicated in behaviors ranging from sullen glares, to whispered accusations, to verbal abuse, to physical assault, the message was clear: "You are butchers and beasts." It took very few of these recognitions for one soldier to realize that "you're not going to get a parade, you're not going to get any pats on the back, you're not going to get anything but spit on and misunderstood and blamed." (*EWH*, p. 256).

The reference group which sponsored *non*-recognition proved to be rather amorphous, consisting of the typical actors in a typical Gemeinschaft. By and large, this group's "silent treatment" of the returning warriors was devoid of malice. In contrast, however, the reference group furnishing recognition was perceived by the vets as deliberately spiteful. This reference group, the anti-war movement or "the Peace People" as the veterans continually refer to them, willfully distorted the soldiers' motives in heeding their country's call to arms. The blatantly non-pacifistic imagery used to describe the actions of this reference group is particularly revealing: "But man, somebody pulled the rug out from under us. Somebody stabbed us in the back. The average person in the Peace struggle didn't understand. *We got stabbed in the back when we got back to the United States by the Peace people* [emphasis added]" (*N*, p. 289). This feeling of having been ruthlessly violated is reiterated throughout the narratives. One memoirist recalls, "M [Company] felt betrayed by all acts of Vietnikism: literally betrayed" (*M*, p. 132).

The source of the "GI as butcherer" recognition was the massive publicity lavished upon the My Lai massacre. The revelations concerning the events in Quang Ngai Province in March, 1968, forever changed the complexion of the Vietnam War in the popular mind. Lt. William "Rusty" Calley personified an identity that came increasingly to be equated with combat duty in Southeast Asia. That identity, popularly construed as both cold-bloodedly inhuman and rabidly bestial, was indiscriminately bestowed upon the veterans primarily by the Peace People. One veteran remembers, "The first time I heard anybody saying, 'Those fucking guys over in Vietnam. Look what they're doing.' Man, it did something to me. Like I was guilty. I was a criminal. You had sentenced me to die" (*N*, p. 288). Another echoes, "People don't understand. They hate you for being there, like you should feel guilty for it. 'You went to Vietnam? Oh, wow, man, where's your head at?' " (*N*, p. 264). A third reports, "The attitude people had to you was you were an asshole for going to Nam in the first place, so fuck you. They would go out of their way to have nothing to do with you" (*N*, p. 304).

This series of identity-generating social recognitions, imputing homocidal dementia to the veterans, was most dramatically enacted in the Gesellschaft public spheres. One soldier reports "walking down the streets of Berkeley . . . everybody was looking at me. All kinds of comments. People spit at me. I was more scared walking down that street than I had been in Vietnam. There I had my weapon and I could protect myself. But they had taken my weapon away. These people looked like they wanted to kill me more than the Vietcong did" (*N*, p. 270). Another, noting opponents of the war were anything but silent on the subject, recalls, "They asked me all kinds of questions. 'How many did you kill? How does it feel to kill somebody?' A hell of a lot better than if he shot me, that's what I told them. . . . Some fucking ass asked me, 'How come you didn't get killed?' " (*N*, p. 268). One frequently cited trauma is hitchhiking, the GI's traditional mode of travel before Vietnam. His identity as "returnee" could make it a nightmare. A soldier standing with his thumb out became a target for vengeful acts by the populace.

He remembered an old troopy jingle as he watched cars whiz by. Doing the impossible. For the ungrateful.
    A bottle flew at him from a passing car and smashed next to his seabag. Somebody in the car yelled something at him. Fascist. Something like that. . . .

They're scared of me. The uniform. He pondered the irony of that. Things don't make any goddamn sense at all. (*FF*, p. 226).

This last sentence, so often heard in the jungles and rice paddies, was now equally appropriate to the world of freeways and supermarkets. As these examples indicate, the soldiers could hardly, in Lifton's lofty phrase, "convey a new dimension of wisdom" to such an unreceptive audience—one that demanded either total silence or tales of genocide. In both instances, the GI was on the losing side in this "deadly game of recognitions."

These conflicting interpretations of the men who fought the war—creatures to be ignored or reviled—insinuated themselves into the vet's consciousness as a single all-encompassing identity: social outcast. Such a "social context of the self" implies "a sense of violated personal and social order, a fundamental break in human connection"[51]—in a word, anomie. The soldiers' anguish in undergoing alternation from knowing survivor to social leper is poignantly rendered in their accounts. One veteran, adopting precisely the language of the classic case of alternation, religious conversion, says, "I got back to the World, but this wasn't the world I had left. I was born again. Like the Christians say, 'Be born again.' I did not fit into the real world anymore. I'm back, but I don't belong. I would have re-upped, but I was all wounded. This world was alienating. . . . People hated GIs for being in the Nam. They was blaming us. I flipped out. I couldn't believe it" (*N*, p. 288). Another describes himself as "overwhelmed with an emotion that was somewhere between a sense of loss and of rebellion" and re-upped hoping that "*something's* gotta be the way you think it's gonna be" (*FF*, p. 231). Thus, reference groups to which they were exposed assigned the vets anomic identities.

In the final portion of this chapter, the consequences of this anomic condition will be explored by supplanting a taken-for-granted psychological explanation with a sociological one, i.e., a theory of past trauma with one of continuing deprivation. Put differently, the soldiers' "disorder" can best be grasped as precisely that: a shattered social order. Our emphasis on the vets' social roles, coupled with the larger culture's belief about them—"that the men returning from [the war] have some-

thing wrong with them that must be tolerated" (*WL*, p. 10)—
demands a reassessment of the affliction from which they pur-
portedly suffer: Post-Vietnam Syndrome.*

Post-Vietnam Syndrome

> You can't translate it or explain it to people. Try to ex-
> plain post-Vietnam syndrome by saying, you know, it's
> trauma. You go through a period of depression. I mean it
> just didn't tell me I lost something. It told me a whole
> bunch of things about myself I probably in some respects
> would be far more successful if I'd never known.
> —*Everything We Had*, p. 131

> On television the Vietnam veteran is always a psycho-
> path who hallucinates and thinks he is in a fire-fight. The
> police and SWAT teams are gentle and patient. Not
> wanting to hurt the veteran who is armed and shouting
> again to his platoon they wait it out and capture him with
> great cleverness. The veteran is led off. He will receive
> the best medical treatment. There are wonderful psychi-
> atrists waiting to help. Some lies are hilarious.
> —*Winners and Losers*, p. 11

The preceding section described how the Vietnam veterans
found themselves caught between incompatible role demands—perpetual silence or compulsory confession—through
the assignment of socially pre-defined identities. Both identities, "invisible man" and "war criminal," represented undesir-
able options within the socially constituted repertoire of
identities in American culture.[52] Both options offered low social status and thereby effectively isolated the individual from
the nomic constructions of society.[53] Thus deprived of the institutional order shielding them against meaninglessness, the

---

*Sometimes called "Post-Traumatic Stress Disorder" or "Delayed Stress Re-
action." All these terms imply nosology. "Post-Vietnam Syndrome" is therefore used generically throughout to refer to any such putatively clinical condition and its corresponding label.

soldiers fell prey to anomie. Put simply, the veterans perceived themselves as tainted and therefore rejected. This perception, structured through and confirmed in ongoing social transactions, rendered the vets' identity as "America's pariahs" subjectively plausible. The purpose of this last section is to indicate how that identity was manifested and socially legitimated.

Despite the specificity of the Post-Vietnam Syndrome (PVS) label, the Vietnam veterans' plight was not without sociological precedent. The onslaught of urbanization at the turn of the century produced "marginal" figures[54] with all the symptoms of Post-Vietnam Syndrome: alcoholism, drug abuse, random violence, antisocial criminality, marital instability.[55] Such behaviors were then subsumed under the rubric "social disorganization."[56] Even more striking is the similarity between the subjective reality reported by the vets and that of another group of war-scarred survivors—the victims who managed to emerge from the rubble of Hiroshima in 1945. Both groups suffer the nearly identical "intro-punitive"[57] affects of depression, rage, apathy, guilt, dread, intense anxiety, and paranoia.* The two sets of witnesses to the awesome destruction inflicted by the American military shared a world view marked by "a vast break-down of faith in the larger human matrix supporting each individual life, and therefore a loss of faith (or trust) in the structure of existence. This shattered existential faith has to do with remaining bound by the image of grotesque and absurd death and equally absurd survival."[58]

Taken out of the language of existential psychiatry, the statement describes a fundamentally anomic meaning system. In more sociological terms, the survivors' world view incorporates recognition of their estrangement from their concrete, historically defined social structure. That the Vietnam veterans' essentially sociological "dis-order" (literally) should be subsumed under the privatizing categories of functional psychiatry is especially unfair. Borrowing from the medical model of individual pathology, Veterans Administration psy-

*We are reminded, in this context, of the remark made by novelist William S. Burroughs: "A paranoid is simply a person in possession of all the facts."

chiatrists used "Post-Vietnam Syndrome" rather early in the war to delineate consistent behavior patterns specific to Vietnam veterans.[59] One psychiatrist, cognizant of the social processes which such a clinical designation obscures, says, "Post-Vietnam Syndrome is a dubious, easily abused category . . . the implication that can often accompany the use of the term is that normal or desirable behavior (in contrast to the post-Vietnam syndrome) would be to adapt quietly to existing American social and war-making arrangements."[60] Chief among those existing social arrangements is the chronic collective amnesia regarding America's longest war and, ipso facto, the symbolic annihilation of the men who waged it. That PVS proves virtually intractable to psychiatric, i.e., privatizing, therapies shouldn't surprise anyone.[61]

Significantly, the soldiers' own understanding of their physical and emotional distress is cast in these terms, implying "a ready equation of effects of war with a clinical condition."[62] One soldier neatly expressed both the subjective reality and the "official" label that purports to explain it: "I felt bad about myself. People treated me funny. I was severely depressed. I could accomplish nothing. This was before they put a label on post-Vietnam syndrome" (N, p. 297). Such testimony emphasizes the importance of the soldiers' post-war attempt to account for their own distress. As our informant confides, they appealed to the socially established psychological theory of Post-Vietnam Syndrome.

More specifically, the veterans' self-conception was structured not only by the face-to-face recognitions bestowed by laymen but also through interpretations administered, often indirectly, by specially trained personnel. The pronouncements of these identity experts (psychologists, psychiatrists, social workers, psychiatric nurses, counselors) trickled down to the layman primarily through the mass media. Consequently, these psychological theories permeated "conversation" in those face-to-face encounters in which identity is socially sustained. In sum, psychological theories, like the functional psychiatric one to which PVS was recently added, "introduce a further dialectic relationship between identity and society—the relationship between psychological theory and those elements it purports to define and explain."[63]

The implications of this relationship reveal important features of the soldiers' world view. Its dialectical structure means that a socially established theory of identity will have socializing effects: "psychologies will produce a reality which in turn serves as the basis for their verification."[64] Because "psychologies pertain to the dimension of reality that is of the most continuous subjective relevance for all individuals . . . the dialectic between theory and reality affects the individual in a palpably direct and intensive manner."[65] Even more than the other legitimating theories we have examined, psychological theories have a "realizing potency."[66]

As an example, consider again the events at Salem, Massachusetts, in 1692. Demonic possession, the socially established psychological theory of the Puritans, increased in frequency as successive cases were reported and treated. Each successful "cure" provided empirical support for the adequacy of the theory. Thus satisfactorily diagnosed and remedied, demonic possession became the only "valid" theory to which sensible men could possibly subscribe. The "truth" of the Puritans' theory of identity, like that of psychoanalysis and its offshoots, rests not upon the ultimate ontological status of its categories but upon the social support the theory receives. In this respect, the Puritans' and the Freudians' categories—possession and obsession respectively—are empirically adequate in the same way. As this example illustrates, "theories of identity are always embedded in more comprehensive theories about reality."[67] A given phenomenon, for instance involuntary muscle spasms, can serve equally as incontrovertible evidence of either devilry or unconscious defenses. The determination will depend only upon whether a larger religious or mechanistic framework is presumed.[68] Put simply, "psychology always presupposes cosmology."[69]

The relationship between psychological theory and identity is relevant precisely because the vets relied on a psychological label to interpret their anomic misery. Unfortunately, their faith in the explanatory power of the label only exacerbated their anomie. The labelling procedure further "privatized"[70] their distress by classifying the effects of anomie—depression, rage, guilt, anxiety, nightmares—as positive evidence of individual abnormality. Rather than employing what C. Wright Mills called the "sociological imagination," American culture exercised its typically "psychological myopia"—translating public issues into private troubles.[71]

In fact, the single PVS "symptom" most frequently reported by the vets and publicized by the media is the display of "unprovoked" anger. This anger, which in a different context would be viewed as justifiable outrage at historical events, is, in the veterans' case, dismissed as an effect of psychological aberration. One commentator wryly observed that "in an article called 'How to Treat a Viet Vet,' *Glamour* warned its readers: 'If you avoid arguments because he's been trained to killing and to anger, and you're afraid of his releasing them on you—another common problem—you've got to talk about it. Chances are he has been afraid of this, too'" (*WL*, p. 10). The remedy for the soldiers' anger, in the popular wisdom expressed by *Glamour*, is a diluted variant of "the talking cure" of psychoanalysis. The implication is that social arrangements, including those which structure public opinion and thereby generate social recognitions, need not be analyzed, only those "unreasonably" angry men. As the commentator notes, "It is almost never suggested in these glossy little pieces that the war was wrong, only that the men returning from it have something wrong with them that must be tolerated" (*WL*, p. 10).

The veterans' own words, however, clarify precisely how inappropriate such a privatizing explanation finally is. One vet says, "There are times which come at me unexpectedly out of the dark when I just absolutely fly off the handle about something and I know it's because of Nam. It is that anger that's triggered. When I encounter something that's really stupid, it's Nam that makes me angry" (*N*, p. 299). Another recalls, "After I had been in Quon Loi for a week or two, I was very angry. I stayed angry almost all the time I was there. I brought that anger home with me like a lot of other men. What I saw angered me" (*N*, p. 142). A third simply asserts, "I stayed angry for at least two years" (*N*, p. 285). It is an especially distorted view which regards the soldiers' anger—"various forms of rage, guilt, and protest which are actually appropriate to the experience"[72]—as a manifestation of psychiatric disease.

The primary intention here is not to affix blame to the mental health professionals who dispensed the wisdom expressed in the clinical term "Post-Vietnam Syndrome." Neither is our purpose to scourge the popular media which circulated simplifications of the health professionals' wisdom and nostrums. Rather, the point is to show how a reference group shapes a perspective on social reality that dialectically realizes itself. Through the communication channels of mass society, identity-repair personnel produced a reality in which virtually all Americans participated and which in turn acted back upon them. One soldier attests to the effects of PVS's incorporation into the culture's stock of knowledge: "That was the first time I noticed that people were treating me funny, like I was a psycho, like a slightly retarded child who had a history of violent outbreaks. 'I want you to be nice, now. You're not going to cause any trouble, are you? We know you've had it rough, but just relax and take it easy'" (*N*, p. 275). Another recalls people treating him as if he "wasn't housebroken. They can't control you" (*N*, p. 304).

These recognitions, although similar to those bestowed upon the veterans by the Peace People, are qualitatively different. The anti-war activists straightforwardly accused the Vietnam warriors of murderous intent, justifying their exclusion from society as moral lepers. The recognition of the soldiers as "victims" of PVS, however, stripped them of all credibility in their efforts to bear witness. As sufferers of a psychiatric disorder, they were automatically judged unreliable. Whatever force their testimony about the Vietnam War and their own actions within it may have had was deflected by the allowances made for their "condition." In short, the "enlightened" attitude of solicitous compassion served to reinforce their self-apprehension as "walking wounded."

This assertion does not mean that such recognitions were entirely groundless. Indeed, more than a few veterans are "possessed."[73] The narratives record the words of at least enough genuine time bombs now wandering the streets to give the stereotype a basis in fact. Tragically, some American boys "got out there and found out that their talent was killing and they were damn good at it. They had a taste of killing and they all like it. Now, when the war ended, what were they going to do?" (*N*, p. 175). One veteran answered that question simply: "When I came back to America, I'll tell you a little secret, I was doing a lot of stick-ups. Because I wanted that *thing*. Stuff didn't bother me, like what happens if you get shot. Fuck that. I been shot. Being in trouble doesn't bother you. Big fucking deal. How bad can it be?" (*N*, p. 301). The "thing" emphasized above is the exhilaration associated with combat. Even the most sober and responsible veterans remember that "high" as extraordinarily powerful. One ex-officer, otherwise horrified by what he did overseas in his country's name, explained that "the rights or wrongs of the war aside, there was a magnetism about combat. You seemed to live more intensely under fire. Every sense was sharper, the mind worked clearer and faster. Perhaps it was the tension of opposites that made it so, an attraction balanced by revulsion, hope that warred with dread. You found yourself on a precarious emotional edge, experiencing a headiness that no drink or drug could match" (*RW*, p. 218). Others, more prosaically, echo such a sentiment: "The adrenaline runs for so long, then it all stops. The war's ending cut you off just like that. You say okay, but the adrenaline is still running" (*EWH*, p. 255); "He dreaded what the rumbling tanks, the sputters of machine guns would bring, but at the same time the very prospect energized him with awe and determination" (*FF*, p. 351). One correspondent remarked, "Some saw the action and declared for it, only heavy killing could make them feel so alive. . . . Every time there was combat you had a license to go maniac, everyone snapped over the line at least once there and nobody noticed, they hardly noticed if you forgot to snap back again" (*D*, p. 58).

These soldiers' desperate exploits were given full media coverage and rendered the "violent vet" image empirically valid. Unfortunately, that image was indiscriminately bestowed upon the veterans. Such recognitions intensified the soldiers' anomie by reinforcing their low social status.

For all the veterans, then, the explanation offered to account for their cognitive difficulties aggravated those difficulties. The diagnosis became itself part of the disease. The result was anomie as a persistent feature of the veterans' biographies. One participant in and survivor of America's sole military defeat offers a poignant conclusion to this study of the vets' post-war careers: "I can't say if I was one of the lucky ones. Sometimes I wish I could have just went ahead and died with my friends. I used to say, 'I'm only dreaming. I'll wake up one day. I will wake up.' But I never woke up" (*EWH*, p. 157).

NOTES

1. Peter Berger and Thomas Luckmann, *The Social Construction of Reality* (New York: Doubleday and Co., 1966), p. 72.

2. Role theory can be traced to the psychological writings of William James. Seminal thinkers in the American sociological tradition include Charles Horton Cooley, *Human Nature and the Social Order* (New York: Scribner and Sons, 1922); and George Herbert Mead, *Mind, Self and Society* (Chicago: University of Chicago Press, 1934). For a thorough analysis of the concept of role for sociological understanding, see Ralf Dahrendorf, "Homo Sociologicus: On the History, Significance, and Limits of the Category of Social Role," in *Essays in the Theory of Society* (Stanford: Stanford University Press, 1968), pp. 19–87.

3. Berger and Luckmann, *The Social Construction of Reality*, p. 56.

4. Tamatso Shibutani, "Reference Groups as Perspectives," *American Journal of Sociology* (1955), p. 567.

5. Peter Berger, *Invitation to Sociology* (New York: Doubleday and Co., 1963), p. 96.

6. Peter Berger, "Identity as a Problem in the Sociology of Knowledge," *European Journal of Sociology* 7 (1966): 105.

7. Ibid., p. 112.

8. Ibid., p. 107.

9. Berger, *Invitation to Sociology*, p. 99.

10. Ibid., p. 98.

11. Berger, "Identity as a Problem in the Sociology of Knowledge," p. 114.

12. Berger, *Invitation to Sociology*, p. 103.

13. Berger, "Identity as a Problem in the Sociology of Knowledge," p. 111.

14. Clifford Geertz's suggestive comment that "the concept of per-

son . . . exists in recognizable form among all social groups" indicates, we believe, the importance of specifying both the pan-cultural processes that confer personhood and the particular variations of "person" empirically available in different cultures. See Clifford Geertz, "From the Native's Point of View: On the Nature of Anthropological Understanding," in *Symbolic Anthropology*, eds. Janet L. Dolgin et al. (New York: Columbia University Press, 1977), pp. 480–92.

15. Goffman distinguishes among five kinds of total institutions on the basis of the kinds of inmates they are designed to serve. There are those for persons felt to be: incapable and harmless; incapable and a threat to the community; an intentional danger to the community; in retreat from the world; and pursuing some work-like task. Our concern with the military falls squarely into this last category which is neither overtly punitive nor expressly designed to impose complete isolation. For a full discussion with examples of each, see Erving Goffman, *Asylums* (New York: Doubleday and Co., 1961), pp. 4–5.

16. Berger, *Invitation to Sociology*, p. 120.

17. Erving Goffman, *The Presentation of Self in Everyday Life* (New York: Doubleday and Co., 1959), p. 11.

18. Gresham M. Sykes, *The Society of Captives: A Study of a Maximum Security Prison* (Princeton: Princeton University Press, 1958).

19. Goffman, *Asylums*, p. 7.

20. Berger, "Identity as a Problem in the Sociology of Knowledge," p. 112.

21. Ibid., p. 111.

22. Peter Berger and Hansfried Kellner, *Sociology Re-Interpreted* (New York: Doubleday and Co., 1981), p. 167.

23. Berger, *Invitation to Sociology*, p. 120.

24. Hans H. Gerth and C. Wright Mills, *Character and Social Structure* (New York: Harcourt, Brace and Co., 1953), pp. 153–58.

25. See A. H. M. Jones, "The Decline and Fall of the Roman Empire," *History*, New Series 40 (1955): 209–26.

26. Peter Berger, "In Praise of Particularity," in *Facing Up to Modernity* (New York: Basic Books, 1977), p. 134.

27. Berger, *Invitation to Sociology*, pp. 96–97.

28. Berger, "In Praise of Particularity," p. 133.

29. After the cessation of hostilities at the end of WWII, the American troops were returned home by ship. Thus, the period of "decompression" could take anywhere from two weeks to six months depending upon the theater of operations to which the GI was assigned. Such a lengthy homecoming had the wholly beneficial effect of per-

mitting gradual role dispossession, re-culturation, and a more pain-less (because incremental) resumption of civilian role scheduling. For an absorbing account of the journey back from what we have throughout described as The Paradigm War, see Paul Fussel, "Hiro-shima: A Soldier's View," *The New Republic*, August 22 and 29, 1981.

30. Goffman, *Asylums*, p. 14.

31. Ibid., p. 15.

32. Berger and Luckmann, *The Social Construction of Reality*, p. 202.

33. Goffman, *Asylums*, p. 13.

34. Berger, *Invitation to Sociology*, p. 106.

35. Ibid.

36. Peter Berger contends that this term is more neutral than "conversion," with the latter's religiously charged overtones, and therefore more suitable for conducting value-free social science. Since 1963, when Berger wrote this, religious-like conversions have reached epidemic proportions among the American middle classes. Mass-ap-peal political and psychological creeds have become part of the stan-dard stock of experience in secular middle-class life. This explosion in the number of available therapies for identity transformation makes the phenomenon of alternation ripe for further study. For the origi-nal formulation, see Berger, *Invitation to Sociology*, p. 51. For fur-ther clarification of that position, see Thomas Luckmann and Peter Berger, "Social Mobility and Personal Identity," *European Journal of Sociology* 5 (1964): 331–44.

37. Shibutani, "Reference Groups as Perspectives," p. 562. The au-thor mentions inconsistency of behavior, juvenile delinquency, social attitudes, status problems, and reactions to mass communications as research areas where reference group theory has been profitably ap-plied.

38. Ibid.

39. Ibid., p. 563.

40. Berger, *Invitation to Sociology*, p. 120.

41. For a provocative discussion of the ways in which mass media communication provides imaginary reference groups, see John Caughey, "Artificial Social Relations in America," *American Quar-terly* 30 (Spring 1978). Within the perspective outlined here it is par-ticularly ironic that we become the "performers" for media figures who are thereby cast in the role of "audience."

42. Shibutani, "Reference Groups as Perspectives," p. 565.

43. Berger, *Invitation to Sociology*, p. 120.

44. Shibutani, "Reference Groups as Perspectives," p. 568.

45. Berger, *Invitation to Sociology*, p. 65.

46. Shibutani, "Reference Groups as Perspectives," p. 568.

47. Robert J. Lifton, *Home from the War* (New York: Simon and Schuster, 1973), p. 26.

48. Ibid., p. 28.

49. Berger, "Identity as a Problem in the Sociology of Knowledge," p. 107.

50. Hunter S. Thompson reports that even the Hell's Angels motorcycle gang benefitted economically from the Vietnam War. Despite their outrageous appearance, criminal records, and rotten reputation, the Angels "were hired in spite of themselves" when their home base, Oakland, California, was "turned into a shipping depot for men and material bound for the Far East." See Hunter Thompson, *Hell's Angels* (Ballantine Books, 1966), p. 314.

51. Marcul R. Stuen, M.D., "The Vietnam Veteran; Characteristics and Needs" Mimeo (VA Hospital, Tacoma, Washington), cited in Lifton, *Home from the War*, p. 36.

52. For an invaluable approach to the problem of classifying identities within a cultural repertoire, see Anthony F. C. Wallace, "Identity Processes in Personality and Culture," in *Cognition, Personality, and Clinical Psychology* (San Francisco: Jossey Bass, 1967); Wallace and Fogelson, "The Identity Struggle," in *Intensive Family Therapy* (New York: Harper and Row, 1965); and John Caughey, "Identity Struggles in the Mental Status Exam" (meetings of the American Anthropological Association, Los Angeles, 1979).

53. "The most consistent empirical correlate of anomie as a measured attitude is low social status." See James T. Borhek and Richard F. Curtis, *A Sociology of Belief* (New York: John Wiley and Sons, 1975), p. 143.

54. Robert Farris, *Chicago Sociology, 1920–1932* (Chicago: University of Chicago Press, 1970). For the historical background of this concern with the anomic consequences of urbanization, see Thomas Haskell, *The Emergence of Professional Social Science* (Champaign, Ill.: University of Illinois Press, 1977).

55. Some 70,000 Vietnam combat vets are now serving sentences in U. S. prisons. The divorce rate among combat vets is twice that of the rest of their generation, and over 20 percent are unemployed. They also have a suicide rate estimated as 23 to 33 percent higher than that of non-veterans. See Philip Caputo, "The Unreturning Army," *Playboy*, January 1982, p. 118.

56. Farris, *Chicago Sociology*, p. 17.

57. Borhek and Curtis, *A Sociology of Belief*, p. 139.

58. Lifton, *Home from the War*, p. 67.

59. Ibid., p. 420.

60. Ibid.

61. Lifton describes one instance wherein the privatizing implication of the psychological theory in which PVS is embedded was explicitly revealed. He says, "Another veteran told of his anger during a parallel encounter with a psychiatrist conducting a group session at a Veterans Administration clinic. During a general discussion of anger, the veteran described the extent of his own rage, only to be told by the therapist: 'But don't you see how all of it is in your head?' " See Lifton, *Home from the War*, p. 166.

62. Lifton, *Home from the War*, p. 420.

63. Berger and Luckmann, *The Social Construction of Reality*, p. 176.

64. Ibid., p. 178.

65. Ibid., p. 176.

66. Ibid., p. 178.

67. Ibid., p. 175.

68. For a fascinating account of the way in which Freud constructed a psychology based on mechanistic assumptions carried over virtually intact from nineteenth-century biology, see Frank J. Sulloway, *Freud: Biologist of the Mind* (New York: Basic Books, 1979), especially pp. 419–95.

69. Berger and Luckmann, *Social Construction of Reality*, p. 175.

70. For a more comprehensive consideration of "privatization," see Thomas Luckmann, *Das Problem der Religion in der modernen Gesellschaft* (Freiburg: Rombach, 1963).

71. C. Wright Mills, *The Sociological Imagination* (New York: Oxford University Press, 1959), p. 8. A provocative discussion of the relationship between the psychological and sociological interpretive schemes appears in Peter L. Berger, "Toward a Sociological Understanding of Psychoanalysis," *Social Research* 32 (1965): 26–41.

72. Lifton, *Home from the War*, p. 186.

73. It is estimated that 10 to 15 percent of the vets are "psychiatric basket cases," i.e., psychotics, drug addicts, incurable alcoholics. See Arthur Egendorf, *Legacies of Vietnam: Comparative Adjustment of Veterans and their Peers* (New York: The New York Center for Policy Research, 1981). The literature on such casualties of modern war is extensive. For an illuminating historical comparison, see John Appell et al., "Comparative Incidence of Neuro-Psychiatric Casualties in WWI and WWII," *American Journal of Psychiatry* 103 (1946–47): 196–99; and S. Schoenberger, "Disorders of the Ego in Wartime,"

British Journal of Medical Psychology 21 (1947–48): 248–53. A discussion of the peculiar challenges of working with Vietnam vets can be found in James F. Veninga, "The Healing Nightmare: A Conversation with Harry Wilmer," *The Texas Humanist* 5 (November–December 1982).

Afterword

Now, war ended, all I am left with are simple, unprofound scraps of truth. Men die. Fear hurts and humiliates. It is hard to be brave. It is hard to know what bravery *is*. Dead human beings are heavy and awkward to carry, things smell different in Vietnam, soldiers are dreamers, drill sergeants are boors, some men thought the war was proper and others didn't and most didn't care. Is that the stuff for a morality lesson, even for a theme?
> —*If I Die in a Combat Zone*, p. 31

Finally, this book ought not to be regarded as protest. Protest arises from a belief that one can change things or influence events. . . . It might, perhaps, prevent the next generation from being crucified in the next war.
> But I don't think so.
> —*A Rumor of War*, p. xxi

More than a decade has passed since the withdrawal of American forces from the Asian peninsula. That withdrawal marked the end of U. S. involvement in a grim episode of our military history. Since that time the nation has embarked on a program of organized mourning—a halting first step in the process of confronting the taint from the Vietnam War. Ironically, such an undertaking actually highlights the tainted nature of the war and the difficulty in purifying it.[1] The controversy surrounding the embodiment of America's anguish—

the Vietnam War Memorials in the nation's capitol—serves as a powerful reminder that paying homage to the fallen of a tainted war requires rituals outside the culture's customary repertoire. At issue in the furor over what shape our material representations of the Vietnam War will take is a subtler, more far-reaching question: What form will our collective memory—our national history—assume in the minds of subsequent generations? Will the twin monuments which political compromise has condoned offer license for any interpretation and thereby constitute an element in a plausibility structure in which every man truly becomes his own historian? If so, the Tainted War will claim victims well into the future.

All fashionable talk of pluralism aside, the survival of a common culture requires at least a minimal consensus about causes and effect, means and motives, premises and possibilities, methods and morals. Because cultural systems must be constrained within proximate limits if they are to retain the cohesion that enables them to persist (become what Kai Erikson labels "boundary maintaining"),[2] pivotal events must be rendered fairly uniformly meaningful. To believe otherwise is sociological folly. As long as the Vietnam War remains "up for grabs" historiographically, and as long as the status of those who fought and those who fled and those who grew fat on its by-products remains undecided, our collective culture suffers.

This concern is not an idle one. Much depends on how a society uses the materials of its historical experience to fashion a self-image.[3] A nation's record in mobilizing for war, acquitting itself in battle, and negotiating the peace are decisive in forging its self-understanding. That self-understanding is (on the level of public awareness at which memorial statues are aimed) clearly a matter of arriving at a single, overarching account—an all-inclusive war story—of what the war meant to a people. This narrative comprises the history a society tells itself and, most importantly, its future members. The Vietnam War story that is currently being fixed in the public mind is peculiar, perhaps unique, in American military lore; it is closer to a modernist literary exercise than a full-blown martial saga. In the style of Henry James rather than George Patton, the Vietnam War fable proposes nuances, demands distance, and questions belief and the willing suspension thereof. What would seem to be determinate and stable features of the "story"—U. S. mendacity, altruism, pitilessness, and paternalism—are being rendered fluid and provisional at best. All efforts to neatly excise the taint from the Tainted War founder on this elusive, Rorschach-like quality of the events in question.

"T'ain't reality and t'ain't a dream"—the opening epigraph from which this study draws its title—is exemplified in the manner in which the war is now remembered as well as in the actual fighting some dozen years ago in which 57,000 Americans lost their lives. Varying amounts of pride, shame, and indifference still inform the collective conscience. Such uncertainty has bred barbarism in the past and may prove to be our undoing in the future.

Examples from the history of the present century abound with catastrophes provoked by such laissez-faire historiography. Most telling in this context is the Germans' understanding of their own misfortunes in the Great War. That understanding, grounded in a comprehensive story of political machinations and betrayals by the "November Criminals," paved the way for the Paradigm War and its attendant inhumanity. The war story Hitler told his defeated countrymen proved plausible initially because it removed the taint. Such a strategy, offering the German people a single, seemingly solid interpretation of World War I, offered a way out of the maze of conflicting and often mutually exclusive versions. Hitler's privileged and authoritative account did one thing that the welter of alternative versions failed to do: it answered questions instead of begging them and did so by denying the taint. An entire world was forced to pay the price for that compelling narrative.

The concern about multiple interpretations of the Vietnam experience is not a dry academic cavil; practical issues hang in the balance. Rearmament, aggression, vulnerability, and defense postures all presuppose the nation has drawn lessons from its recent past. We can view the Tainted War as a noble crusade and, in so doing, remove the taint. Similarly, we can regard it as a tragic, albeit well-intentioned, error and thereby

mitigate it. Finally, we can insist on the moral failure which
caused it and therein preserve its contaminated status as an
object lesson for future generations.

Drawing a lesson from the Vietnam War requires more than
performing a belated act of mourning for the dead. The dead
have no say anymore. What happened and how it ought to be
regarded is beyond their abilities to bear witness, but the living and the yet unborn will be called on to bear that witness.
We must "make our peace" with the war. To do this requires
more than speaking up. It requires listening. Our hope is that
this study will be viewed as an attempt, tentative and incom-
plete, to do just that. Our vacillation as a culture between hope
and helplessness, compassion and complacency, forgiveness and
forgetting is a symptom of our readiness to insist on removing
or preserving a taint that we have prejudged rather than
reckoned with. It is our hope that the politicians and profit-
eers and persistently silent majority will stop to consider the
story of the Vietnam War they shall tell each other and be-
queath to the inhabitants of the future. It is only by so doing
that the conclusion of one veteran war-watcher will be refuted
and our questions—and prayers—come to matter at all:

As I watch the reactions, I realize that as a country, we learned
nothing from Vietnam. A few—a small group in this massive country—have been driven mad by Vietnam. And the rest of the country
has learned nothing. (*WL*, p. 33)

NOTES

1. Mary Tew Douglas, *Purity and Danger: An Analysis of Concepts
of Pollution and Taboo* (New York: Praeger, 1966).

2. Kai T. Erikson, *Wayward Puritans* (New York: John Wiley and
Sons, 1966).

3. Gene Wise, *American Historical Explanations* (Homewood, Ill.:
Dorsey Press, 1973).

Bibliography

Vietnam War Narratives: Primary Sources

Baker, Mark. *Nam: The Vietnam War in the Words of the Men and Women Who Fought There*. New York: William Morrow, 1981.

Bryan, C. D. B. *Friendly Fire: A Non-Fiction Novel*. New York: G. P. Putnam's Sons, 1976.

Caputo, Philip. *A Rumor of War*. New York: Ballantine Books, 1977.

Downs, Frederick. *The Killing Zone: My Life in the Vietnam War*. New York: W. W. Norton and Co., 1978.

Duncan, Donald. *The New Legions*. New York: Random House, 1967.

Emerson, Gloria. *Winners and Losers: Battles, Retreats, Gains, Losses, and Ruins from a Long War*. New York: Random House, 1976.

Glasser, Ronald. *365 Days*. New York: G. Braziller, 1971.

Halberstam, David. *One Very Hot Day*. Boston: Houghton Mifflin Co., 1967.

Hasford, Gustav. *The Short-Timers*. New York: Harper and Row, 1979.

Herr, Michael. *Dispatches*. New York: Alfred A. Knopf, 1978.

Karlin, Wayne; Paquet, Basil T.; and Rottman, Larry, eds. *Free-Fire Zone: Short Stories by Vietnam Veterans*. New York: McGraw-Hill, 1973.

Klinkowitz, Jerome, and Somer, John, eds. *Writing Under Fire: Stories of the Vietnam War*. New York: Delta Books, 1978.

Lane, Mark. *Conversations with Americans*. New York: Simon and Schuster, 1970.

Lang, Daniel. *Casualties of War*. New York: McGraw-Hill, 1969.

Lifton, Robert J. *Home from the War*. New York: Simon and Schuster, 1973.

O'Brien, Tim. *Going after Cacciato.* New York: Dell, 1975.
———. *If I Die in a Combat Zone, Box Me Up and Ship Me Home.* New York: Delacorte Press, 1979.
Sack, John. *M.* New York: New American Library, 1966.
Santoli, Al. *Everything We Had: An Oral History of the Vietnam War by Thirty-three American Soldiers Who Fought There.* New York: Random House, 1981.
Webb, James. *Fields of Fire.* New York: Bantam Books, 1978.

Vietnam War Narratives: Auxiliary Sources

Adler, Bill. *Letters from Vietnam.* New York: Dutton, 1967.
Anderson, Charles R. *Vietnam: The Other War.* Novato, Calif.: Presidio Press, 1982.
Associated Press. *The Eyewitness History of the Vietnam War: 1961–1975.* Associated Press, 1984.
Baer, Gordan and Howell-Koehler, Nancy. *Vietnam: The Battle Comes Home.* Dobbs Ferry, N.Y.: Morgan, 1984.
Berrigan, Daniel. *Night Flight to Hanoi.* New York: Macmillan, 1968.
Bisignano, Flavio. *Vietnam—Why?: An American Citizen Looks at the War.* Torrance, Calif.: Frank Publishing, 1968.
Boyle, Richard. *The Flower of the Dragon: The Breakdown of the U. S. Army in Vietnam.* San Francisco: Ramparts Press, 1972.
Briscoe, Edward G. *Diary of a Short-Timer in Vietnam.* New York: Vantage Press, 1970.
Bronfman, Fred. *Voices from the Plain of Jars.* New York: Harper and Row, 1972.
Clark, Johnnie M. *Guns Up!* New York: Ballantine, 1984.
Coe, Charles. *Young Man in Vietnam.* New York: Four Winds Press, 1972.
Daly, James A. *A Hero's Welcome.* Indianapolis: Bobbs-Merrill, 1975.
Dedra, Don. *Anybody Here from Arizona?: A Look at the Vietnam War.* Phoenix: The Arizona Republic, 1966.
Delvecchio, John. *13th Valley.* New York: Bantam Books, 1982.
Dengler, Dieter. *Escape from Laos.* New York: Zebra, 1982.
Dodge, Ed. *Dau: A Novel of Vietnam.* New York: Macmillan Publishing Co., 1984.
Donlan, Roger H. *Outpost of Freedom.* New York: McGraw-Hill, 1965.
Dougan, Clark and Weiss, Stephen. *Nineteen Sixty-Eight, Vol. 6.* Manning, Robert L., ed. (The Vietnam Experience Series) Boston: Boston Publishing Co., 1982.

Doyle, Edward G. and Lipsman, Samuel L. *America Takes Over, Vol. 4*. Manning, Robert, L., ed. (The Vietnam Experience Series) Boston: Boston Publishing Co., 1982.

Drury, Richard. *My Secret War*. Fallbrook: Aero Publishers, 1979.

Dudman, Richard. *Forty Days with the Enemy*. New York: Liveright, 1971.

Ehrhart, W. D. *Vietnam-Perkasie: A Combat Marine Memoir*. Jefferson, N.C.: McFarland and Co., 1983.

Falabello, Robert J. *Vietnam Memoirs*. New York: McGraw-Hill, 1970.

Fall, Bernard B. *Viet-Nam Witness*. New York: Praeger, 1966.

Flood, Charles Barcelen. *The War of the Innocents*. New York: McGraw-Hill, 1970.

Garland, A. N., ed. *Combat Notes from Vietnam*. Infantry Magazine, Fort Benning, Ga., 1968.

Greene, Felix. *Vietnam! Vietnam!* Palo Alto, Calif.: Fulton Publishing Co., 1966.

Hawthorne, Lesleyanne. *Refugee: The Vietnamese Experience*. New York: Oxford University Press, 1982.

Herbert, Anthony. *Soldier*. New York: Holt, Rinehart and Winston, 1973.

Herrington, Stuart A. *Peace with Honor? An American Reports on Vietnam, 1973–1975*. Novato, Calif.: Presidio Press, 1983.

Johnson, Raymond W. *Postmark*. Old Tappan, N.J.: Revell, 1968.

Jones, James. *Viet Journal*. New York: McGraw-Hill, 1969.

Joyner et al. *Vietnam Heroes: That We Have Peace, Vol. III*. Topham, J., ed. American Poetry and Literature, 1983.

Just, Ward S. *To What End?: Report from Vietnam*. Boston: Houghton Mifflin, 1968.

Kerry, John. *The New Soldier*. New York: Macmillan, 1971.

Klein, Joe. *Payback: Five Marines after Vietnam*. New York: Knopf, 1984.

Kovic, Ron. *Born on the Fourth of July*. New York: McGraw-Hill, 1976.

Linedecker, Clifford. *Kerry: Agent Orange and an American Family*. New York: St. Martin, 1982.

Little, Loyd. *Parthian Shot*. New York: Viking Press, 1973.

Luce, Don. *Viet Nam: The Unheard Voices*. Ithaca: Cornell University Press, 1969.

McAuley, Anna K. *Miles from Home*. AKLM Publishers, 1984.

MacPherson, Myra. *Long Time Passing: Vietnam and the Haunted Generation*. Garden City, N.Y.: Doubleday, 1984.

McQuinn, Donald E. *Targets*. New York: Tor, 1980.

Maitland, Terrence and McInerney, Peter. *A Contagion of War: Vol.*

5 (1965–1967). Manning, Robert L., ed. (The Vietnam Experience Series) Boston: Boston Publishing Co., 1983.

Mason, Robert. *Chickenhawk*. New York: Viking, 1983.

Meshad, Shad. *Captain for Dark Mornings*. Hendrix, Kathleen, ed. Great Image Associates, 1982.

Ngan, Nguyen, N. and Richey, E. E. *The Will of Heaven: The Story of One Vietnamese and the End of His World*. New York: Dutton, 1982.

Nguyen, Thi-Dinh. *No Other Road to Take*. Ithaca: Cornell University Press, 1976.

Nguyen-cao-Ky. *Twenty Years and Twenty Days*. New York: Stein and Day, 1976.

O'Connor, John James. *A Chaplain Looks at Vietnam*. Cleveland: World Publishing, 1968.

Page, Tim. *Tim Page's Nam*. New York: Knopf, 1983.

Palmer, Dave R. *Summons of the Trumpet*. New York: Ballantine, 1984.

Parks, David. *GI Diary*. New York: Harper and Row, 1968.

Parrish, John Anthony. *A Doctor's Year in Vietnam*. Baltimore: Penguin Books, 1973.

Pick, Michael R. *Childhood-Namhood-Manhood: The Writings of Michael Robert Pick, a Vietnam Veteran*. Pizzito Limited Press, 1982.

Ransom, Robert C. *Letters from Vietnam*. Bronxville, N.Y.: 1968.

Reed, David E. *Upfront in Vietnam*. New York: Funk and Wagnalls, 1967.

Risner, Robinson. *The Passing of the Night: My Seven Years as a Prisoner of the North Vietnamese*. New York: Random House, 1973.

Rowan, Stephan A. *They Wouldn't Let Us Die*. Middle Village, N.Y.: J. David Publishers, 1973.

Rowe, James N. *Five Years to Freedom*. Boston: Little, Brown, 1971.

Salisbury, Harrison Evans. *Behind the Lines*. New York: Harper and Row, 1967.

Schanzenbach, Douglas T. *Vietnam: My Recollections and Reflections*. Pownal, Vt.: Garden Way Publishing, 1983.

Sheehan, Susan. *Ten Vietnamese*. New York: Holt, Rinehart and Winston, 1977.

Shepard, Elaine. *The Doom Pussy*. New York: Trident Press, 1967.

Smith, George Edward. *POW: Two Years with the Viet Cong*. Berkeley: Ramparts Press, 1971.

Snepp, Frank. *Decent Interval: An Insider's Account of Saigon's Indecent End*. New York: Random House, 1977.

Steer, John L. and Dudley, Cliff. *Vietnam: Curse or Blessing?* New Leaf, 1982.

Steinbeck, John. *In Touch.* New York: Knopf, 1969.

Stockdale, Jim and Stockdale, Sybil. *In Love and War: The Story of a Family's Ordeal and Sacrifice During the Vietnam War.* New York: Harper and Row, 1984.

Tregaskis, Richard W. *Vietnam Diary.* New York: Holt, Rinehart and Winston, 1963.

Tucker, James Guy. *Arkansas Men at War.* Little Rock: Arkansas Pioneer Press, 1968.

Vance, Samuel. *The Courageous and the Proud.* New York: W. W. Norton, 1970.

Van Devanter, Lynda and Morgan, Christopher. *Home before Morning: The Story of an Army Nurse in Vietnam.* New York: Beaufort Books, 1983.

Vo Nguyen Giap. *Unforgettable Months and Years.* Ithaca: Cornell University Press, 1975.

Webb, Kate. *On the Other Side: 23 Days with the Viet Cong.* New York: Quadrangle Books, 1972.

West, F. J., Jr. *The Village.* New York: Harper and Row, 1972.

Westmoreland, William Childs. *A Soldier Reports.* Garden City, N.Y.: Doubleday, 1976.

Whitmore, Terry. *Memphis, Nam, Sweden: The Autobiography of a Black American Exile.* Garden City, N.Y.: Doubleday, 1971.

Williams, Craig. *Vietnam, Twelve Months, Twelve Years: An Account of Combat and Readjustment.* Mill Valley, Calif.: Orenda Unity, 1983.

Young, Perry Deane. *Two of the Missing: A Reminiscence of Some Friends in the War.* New York: Avon Books, 1975.

General Sources

Aberle, D. F., et al. "The Functional Prerequisites of a Society." *Ethics* 60 (January 1950): 100–11.

Appell, John, et al. "Comparative Incidence of Neuro-Psychiatric Casualties in WWI and WWII." *American Journal of Psychiatry* 109 (1946–47).

Berger, Peter L. *Facing up to Modernity: Excursions in Society, Politics and Religion.* New York: Basic Books, 1977.

———. *The Heretical Imperative: Contemporary Possibilities of Religious Affirmation.* Garden City, N.Y.: Anchor Press, 1979.

———. *Invitation to Sociology.* Garden City, N.Y.: Doubleday and Co., 1963.

————. *A Rumor of Angels: Modern Society and the Rediscovery of the Supernatural*. Garden City, N.Y.: Doubleday and Co., 1969.

Berger, Peter L.; Berger, Brigette; and Kellner, Hansfried. *The Homeless Mind: Modernization and Consciousness*. New York: Random House, 1973.

Berger, Peter L., and Kellner, Hansfried. *Sociology Re-Interpreted: An Essay on Method and Vocation*. Garden City, N.Y.: Anchor Press, 1981.

Berger, Peter L., and Luckmann, Thomas. *The Social Construction of Reality: A Treatise in the Sociology of Knowledge*. Garden City, N.Y.: Doubleday and Co., 1966.

————. "Social Mobility and Personal Identity." *European Journal of Sociology* 7 (1966): 105–15.

Berger, Peter L., and Neuhaus, Richard J. *To Empower People: The Role of Mediating Structures in Public Policy*. Washington, D.C.: American Enterprise Institute for Public Policy, 1977.

Berger, Peter L., and Pullberg, Stanley. "Reification and the Sociological Critique of Consciousness." *History and Theory* 4 (1964): 196–211.

————. "Toward a Sociological Understanding of Psychoanalysis." *Social Research* 32 (1965): 26–41.

Bohannon, P. *Law and Warfare: Studies in the Anthropology of Conflict*. Garden City, N.Y.: Doubleday and Co., 1969.

Borhek, James T., and Curtis, Richard F. *A Sociology of Belief*. New York: John Wiley and Sons, 1975.

Braestrup, Peter. "Vietnam as the Past." *The Wilson Quarterly* 7 (Summer 1983): 95–139.

Butterfield, Fox. "The New Vietnam Scholarship." *New York Times Magazine*, February 13, 1983.

Caputo, Philip. "The Unreturning Army." *Playboy*, January, 1982.

Carpenter, Edmund, and McLuhan, Marshall. *Explorations in Communication*. Boston: Beacon Press, 1960.

Caughey, John. "Artificial Social Relations in America." *American Quarterly* 30 (Spring 1978).

————. "Identity Struggles in the Mental Status Exam." Meetings of the American Anthropological Association, Los Angeles, 1979.

————. "Personal Identity and Social Organization." *Ethos* 8 (1980).

Cooley, Charles Horton. *Human Nature and the Social Order*. New York: Scribner and Sons, 1922.

Cousins, A. "The Sociology of the War Novel." *Indiana Journal of Social Research* 2 (July 1961): 83–90.

Dahrendorf, Ralf. *Essays in the Theory of Society*. Stanford: Stanford University Press, 1968.

Donellan, Keith. "Speaking of Nothing." *Philosophical Review* 83 (1974).

Douglas, Mary. *Purity and Danger: An Analysis of Concepts of Pollution and Taboo*. New York: Praeger, 1966.

Durkheim, Emile. *Suicide*. New York: The Free Press, 1951.

Egendorf, Arthur. *Legacies of Vietnam: Comparative Adjustment of Veterans and Their Peers*. New York: The New York Center of Policy Research, 1981.

Eliade, Mircea. *Rites and Symbols of Initiation*. New York, 1958.

Erikson, Kai T. *Wayward Puritans*. New York: John Wiley and Sons, 1966.

Farris, Robert. *Chicago Sociology, 1920–1932*. Chicago: University of Chicago Press, 1970.

Ford, Julienne. *Paradigms and Fairy Tales: An Introduction to the Science of Meanings*. London: Routledge and Kegan Paul, 1975.

Fornari, F. *The Psychoanalysis of War*. Garden City, N.Y.: Doubleday and Co., 1974.

Fried, Morton, et al. *War: The Anthropology of Armed Aggression*. Garden City, N.Y.: Natural History Press, 1968.

Frye, Northrop. *Fables of Identity: Studies in Poetic Mythology*. New York: Harcourt, Brace and World, 1963.

Fussell, Paul. *The Great War and Modern Memory*. New York: Oxford University Press, 1975.

Geertz, Clifford. "Blurred Genres." *American Scholar* (Summer 1980), pp. 165–79.

———. "From the Native's Point of View: On the Nature of Anthropological Understanding." In *Symbolic Anthropology*. Edited Janet L. Dolgin, et al. New York: Columbia University Press, 1977.

———. *The Interpretation of Cultures*. New York: Basic Books, 1973.

Gerth, Hans H., and Mills, C. Wright. *Character and Social Structure*. New York: Harcourt, Brace and Co., 1953.

Goffman, Erving. *Asylums*. New York: Doubleday and Co., 1961.

———. *The Presentation of Self in Everyday Life*. New York: Doubleday and Co., 1959.

Halberstam, David. *The Best and the Brightest*. New York: Harper and Row, 1969.

Haskell, Thomas S. *The Emergence of Professional Social Science*. Champaign: University of Illinois Press, 1977.

Herring, George C. *America's Longest War: The United States and Vietnam, 1950–1975*. New York: John Wiley and Sons, 1979.

Hess, Gary. "The First American Commitment in Indochina." *Diplomatic History* 2 (Fall 1978).

Hirsch, E. D. *The Aims of Interpretation*. Chicago: University of Chicago Press, 1976.

Holsti, Ole R., and Rosenau, James. "Vietnam, Consensus, and the Belief Systems of American Leaders." *World Politics* 32 (October 1979): 1–56.

Jones, A. H. M. "The Decline and Fall of the Roman Empire." *History*, New Series, 40 (1955): 209–26.

Karpe, Richard, and Schap, Isidore. "Nostopathy: A Study of Pathogenic Homecoming." *American Journal of Psychiatry* 109 (1952–53): 46–51.

Kelly, R. Gordon. "Literature and the Historian." *American Quarterly* 27 (Spring 1974): 141–59.

———. *Mother Was a Lady*. Westport, Conn.: Greenwood Press, 1974.

King, Chen. "Hanoi's Three Decisions and the Escalation of the Vietnam War." *Political Science Quarterly* 90 (Summer 1975): 239–59.

Kinnard, Douglas. *The War Managers*. Hanover, N.H.: University Press of New England, 1977.

Lazarsfeld, Paul F., and Merton, Robert K. "Mass Communication, Popular Taste, and Organized Social Action." In *Mass Culture: The Popular Arts in America*. Edited Bernard Rosenberg and David Manning White. New York: Van Nostrand Reinhold, 1957.

Leed, Eric J. *No Man's Land: Combat and Identity in World War I*. Cambridge: Cambridge University Press, 1979.

Lefeber, Walter. "The Last War, the Next War, and the New Revisionists." *Democracy* 1 (January 1981): 93–103.

———. "Roosevelt, Churchill, and Indochina, 1942–1945." *American Historical Review* 80 (1975): 1277–95.

Littauer, Ralph, and Norman Uphoff. *The Air War in Indochina*. Boston: Beacon Press, 1972.

Luckmann, Thomas. *Das Problem der Religion in der modernen Gesellschaft*. Freiburg: Rombach, 1963.

Mannheim, Karl. *Ideology and Utopia*. London: Routledge and Kegan Paul, 1936.

Mead, George Herbert. *Mind, Self, and Society*. Chicago: University of Chicago Press, 1934.

Merton, Robert K. *Social Theory and Social Structure*. Chicago: Free Press of Glencoe, 1957.

Mills, C. Wright. *The Sociological Imagination*. New York: Oxford University Press, 1959.

Natanson, Maurice. *Philosophy of the Social Sciences*. New York: Random House, 1963.

Nisbett, Robert. *The Sociology of Emile Durkheim*. New York: Oxford University Press, 1974.

Parsons, Talcott. *The Structure of Social Action*. New York: McGraw-Hill, 1937.

Peterson, Richard A. *The Production of Culture*. Beverly Hills: Sage, 1976.

Plato. *The Dialogues*. Trans. Benjamin Jowett. Oxford: Clarendon Press, 1953.

Real, Michael. "Media Theory: Contributions to an Understanding of American Mass Communications." *American Quarterly* 32 (1980): 238–58.

Rorty, Richard. "Is There a Problem about Fictional Discourse?" In *The Consequences of Pragmatism*. Minneapolis: Minnesota University Press, 1982.

Rosenberg, Bernard, and White, David Manning. *Mass Culture: The Popular Arts in America*. New York: Van Nostrand Reinhold, 1957.

Schoenberger, S. "Disorders of the Ego in Wartime." *British Journal of Medical Psychology* 21 (1947–48): 248–53.

Schutz, Alfred. *The Problem of Social Reality*. The Hague: Nijhoff, 1962.

Searle, John R. "The Logical Status of Fictional Discourse." *New Literary History* 6 (1975): 318–22.

Shibutani, Tamatso. "Reference Groups as Perspectives." *American Journal of Sociology*, 1955.

Sipes, R. "War, Sports, and Aggression: An Empirical Test of Rival Theories." *American Anthropologist* 75 (February 1973): 64–86.

Smith, J. Maynard. "The Evolution of Alarm Calls." In *Readings in Sociobiology*. Edited T. H. Clutton Brock and Paul H. Harvey. San Francisco: W. H. Freeman and Co., 1978.

Starry, Donn A. *Armored Combat in Vietnam*. New York: Arno Press, 1980.

Suid, Lawrence Howard. "The Film Industry and the Vietnam War." (Ph.D. dissertation, Case Western-Reserve, 1980.)

———. *Guts and Glory: Great American War Movies*. Menlo Park, Calif.: Addison Wesley, 1978.

Sulloway, Frank J. *Freud: Biologist of the Mind*. New York: Basic Books, 1979.

Sykes, Gresham M. *The Society of Captives: A Study of a Maximum Security Prison*. Princeton: Princeton University Press, 1958.

Taylor, Sanda. "Teaching the Vietnam War." *The History Teacher* 15 (November 1981): 57–66.

Taylor, Sanda, and Casillas, Rex. "Dealing with Defeat: Teaching the

Vietnam War." *SHAFR Newsletter* 11 (December 1980): 10–18.

Taylor, Telford. *Nuremberg and Vietnam: An American Tragedy*. New York: Quadrangle Books, 1970.

Thompson, Hunter S. *Hell's Angels*. New York: Ballantine Books, 1966.

Thucydides. *The Peloponnesian Wars*. Trans. John H. Finley, Jr. New York: Random House, 1951.

Veninga, James F. "The Healing Nightmare: A Conversation with Harry Wilmer." *The Texas Humanist* 5 (November/December 1982).

Waddell, Dewey, and Wood, Norm. *Air War—Vietnam*. New York: Arno Press, 1978.

Wallace, A. F. C. "Identity Processes in Personality and Culture." *Cognition, Personality, and Clinical Psychology*. San Francisco: Josey Bass, 1967.

———. "Psychological Preparations for War." In *War: The Anthropology of Armed Aggression*. Edited Morton Fried, Marvin Harris, and Robert Murphey. Garden City, N.Y.: The Natural History Press, 1968.

Wasserstrom, Richard. "The Laws of War." In *The Abdication of Philosophy*. Edited Eugene Freeman. La Salle, Ill.: Open Court, 1976.

Wise, Gene. *American Historical Explanations*. Homewood, Ill.: Dorsey Press, 1973.

Young, Marilyn. "Revisionists Revised: The Case of Vietnam." *SHAFR Newsletter* 10 (June 1979): 1–10.

Index